Contents

Book map

	Unit	Unit essay	Skills and language focus
1	**Introduction to academic writing** No source text	*(Reflective questionnaire*)*	■ Reflecting on the process of academic writing
2	**Sustainable energy** **2a** Using waste, Swedish city cuts its fossil fuel use (1) **2b** Using waste, Swedish city cuts its fossil fuel use (2)	*How can alternative sources of energy be harnessed effectively?*	Getting started: ■ Planning an essay ■ Writing a first draft of an essay ■ Peer evaluation of a first draft ■ Incorporating sources ■ Writing introductions
3	**The business of science** **3a** Stop selling out science to commerce **3b** Is business bad for science?	*Over the past 20 years, commercial influences on scientific research have become increasingly detrimental. Discuss.*	Organizing and supporting ideas: ■ Generating ideas for an essay ■ Organizing ideas ■ Incorporating and referencing sources ■ Using paragraph leaders to help organization
4	**Telemedicine** **4c** Telemedicine	**Timed essay:** *As technology continues to improve, the range of potential uses for telemedicine will increase. Telemedicine will offer more beneficial applications in preventing rather than curing disease. Discuss.*	Writing in examinations: ■ Understanding key instruction verbs in examination questions ■ Interpreting examination questions ■ Writing an examination essay
5	**Food security** **5a** Diet and sustainability **5b** The challenge of feeding 9 billion people **5c** Closing the yield gap **5d** Dealing with the situation	*There are many threats to global food supplies. Explain the problem, identify possible solutions, and assess the implications of implementing these solutions.*	The SPSIE approach to organization: ■ Organizing ideas using the SPSIE approach ■ Concluding sentences in paragraphs ■ Writing conclusions

*There is no essay for Unit 1, instead students complete an introductory, reflective questionnaire.

i Introduction

Aims of the course

The purpose of this book is to help students develop the academic writing skills they need to deal effectively with the written element of their academic study, as well as to develop other important skills such as reading research and critical thinking.

New edition

The major change made for the new edition is the change in the topics of the writing tasks, as a result of there being new texts in the *EAS: Reading & Writing Source Book:* the essay titles are all new, except for Unit 4, the unit on writing in examinations. As before, the topics of the texts in the Source Book form the springboard for ideas that can be used in the related essay. Feedback from users of the previous editions has led to other changes, such as extra tasks on incorporating sources into writing, and revisions to the order of some of the microskills. Recent literature on academic writing has also influenced some of the changes.

Principles and approach

Writing is often perceived to be the most complex of all the EAP skills to teach. This view is not without reason, as not only does writing itself encompass so many different processes and skills, but the effective teaching of it demands an understanding of these, as well as an engaging methodological delivery that enables students to assimilate the skills and develop as writers. As Friedrich (2008) says, 'When it comes to teaching academic writing, so many are the possible paths and pedagogical avenues that the newcomer may feel overwhelmed and intimidated.' (p. 1). It would be fair to add that even the experienced teacher may continue to be overwhelmed, although less intimidated, by the efforts required to meet the individual needs of the students in his or her class. It is hoped that this book can help to mitigate such feelings by offering a pathway through academic writing instruction that is staged both for teacher and student, and in which skills are recycled and consolidated to form a solid foundation for effective academic writing at university level.

Although the debate continues about the stage at which students can develop their writing skills in English for Specific Purposes, the focus in this book is English for General Academic Purposes (EGAP), i.e., skills, text types and language forms for Academic English which can be presented to any student (Etherington, 2008). It is felt that in an early developmental stage, students need to focus on the generic aspects of academic writing (such as academic style, neutrality of tone, use of evidence and argument, reference to other texts and authors, and general text organizational patterns) before being able to make the transition to a more specific genre. In addition, it is common for teachers to find themselves in front of classes composed of students intending to study on many different university programmes, thus necessitating a more generic approach. Much of the literature supports this view.

Hyland (2002) makes a convincing case for EGAP and claims the strongest argument is given in Bloor and Bloor's (1986) 'common core hypothesis', suggesting that the common aspects can be taught. Both Currie (1993) and Johns (1997) have supporting arguments, respectively, concerning the existence of generalizable skills and common features of academic prose. Both Zamel and Spack (1998) and Leki (1995) are in agreement. Further arguments, as supported by Etherington, are that lower-level EAP students still need to focus on the basic tools of the language, such as spelling, vocabulary, language structures and use, before being able to write effectively in their subject area. Thus, at various stages of the book, suggestions are included for contextualizing such language development within the tasks.

An integrated approach

At the beginning of the course, it is useful to go over the approach with the students so that they understand the rationale behind the teaching activities. This introduction to the Teacher's Book relates some of the principles mentioned in the student's introduction to the literature on English for Academic Purposes (EAP) writing. The methodology for the first edition of *EAS: Writing* was partly based on an extensive literature review by Richards (1999); reference is still made to this, as well as to more recent literature which was explored when revising the tasks for the current edition. Explicit links can therefore be found to explain why students are asked to engage in certain activities.

Students in a higher-level group can be asked to read through the introduction to the Course Book in their own time, and then be given time in class for a plenary discussion of any questions or issues arising. Students in a lower-level group may need a more step-by-step reading of the introduction, and you may wish to produce some activities for them to use in conjunction with it.

You will find that students relate more closely to the contents of the introduction after they complete the tasks. You should therefore encourage them to refer to the introduction throughout the course.

EAS: Writing has been designed so that it can be used as an integrated course alongside *EAS: Reading* – in the same series – or can be used as an independent writing course. However, even if *EAS: Writing* is used independently, students will still be expected to carry out background reading for the writing topics. It is for this reason that the writing course comes with reading source material in the Source Book, which also contains the reading texts for *EAS: Reading*.

A major reason for supporting an integrated approach to writing is that this responds to the results of research on the development of students' critical thinking skills. A glance at the descriptors used in the Framework for Higher Education Qualifications (FHEQ) will demonstrate the importance given to this aspect of student skills development. The levels of qualification are: Certificate (level 4), Intermediate (level 5), Honours (level 6), Master's (level 7) and Doctoral (level 8). The following table gives examples of descriptors relating to critical thinking for each level.

Level	Example of descriptors relating to critical thinking
4	Holders of the qualification will be able to: ■ evaluate the appropriateness of different approaches to solving problems related to their area(s) of study or work ■ communicate the results of their study/work accurately and reliably, and with structured and coherent arguments
5	Holders of the qualification will be able to: ■ use a range of established techniques to initiate and undertake critical analysis of information, and to propose solutions to problems arising from that analysis ■ effectively communicate information, arguments and analysis in a variety of forms, to specialist and non-specialist audiences, and deploy key techniques of the discipline effectively
6	Holders of the qualification will be able to: ■ critically evaluate arguments, assumptions, abstract concepts and data (that may be incomplete) to make judgements and to frame appropriate questions to achieve a solution – or identify a range of solutions, to a problem
7	Holders of the qualification will be able to: ■ deal with complex issues both systematically and creatively, make sound judgements in the absence of complete data, and communicate their conclusions clearly to specialist and non-specialist audiences
8	Holders of the qualification will be able to: ■ make informed judgements on complex issues in specialist fields, often in the absence of complete data, and be able to communicate their ideas and conclusions clearly and effectively to specialist and non-specialist audiences

In order for international students to be fully prepared for their future study environments, and for their competence in English to be developed, students need to be introduced to the conventions peculiar to academic study in English-speaking universities. They also need training in skills that will allow them to function successfully in terms of these conventions, especially with regard to academic writing. Such conventions include critical analysis and argument in extended academic writing, and acknowledgement of the sources of ideas. Many students who come to study in the UK come from cultural and academic backgrounds in which they are not required to criticize the works of others or to formulate their own arguments with the aid of well-founded supporting evidence. Consequently, such students may not be fully aware of the level of critical analysis and argument required in academic writing for postgraduate-level study in English-speaking universities. Furthermore, there may be some reluctance to engage in tasks that encourage such levels of critical thinking. Ideally, such students should undergo a period of transition in which they are introduced to the 'new' academic culture. Therefore, EAP teaching material should include tasks and activities that train students to develop their critical thinking skills.

EAP research supports an integrated approach to the teaching of reading and writing. Critical thinking is viewed by Carson and Leki (1993) as 'the ability to transform information for their own [students'] purposes in reading and to synthesize their prior knowledge with another text in writing … Together, reading and writing facilitate the development of critical thinking' (p. 100). Similarly, Belcher and Browne (1995) define critical thinking as 'responding in an evaluative, analytical way to texts' (p. 135). Grabe & Kaplan (1996) assert that an ideal writing course would 'present topical issues and writing tasks which motivate and engage students, while at the same time being challenging and providing opportunities for learning' (p. 262). The implications of research for the teaching of academic writing are that there should be provision for an integrated skills approach which includes the specific development of critical thinking skills.

Course structure

Each unit of *EAS: Writing* has a writing topic based on the corresponding reading text in the Source Book. This follows the principle that students will read an academic text for a particular purpose on their academic course. One of the main purposes of the source texts is to provide students with information they can use to support their ideas in their written assignments. They process and critically analyze that information, before incorporating it into their own argument; thus, they engage in a problem-solving activity. It is important to reflect this process on an academic writing programme.

Task design

The tasks and activities have been designed so that students can develop the different aspects of their writing (as stated in the introduction to the Course Book), and develop effective strategies for approaching a writing task in carefully scaffolded stages. Scaffolding involves breaking down large tasks into smaller ones, with a clear indication of the steps involved in this process, and using questioning techniques to guide students towards task completion. It also involves identifying, teaching, developing and reviewing strategies which students can employ for different types of tasks and activities (Bruner, 1983). This approach reflects research findings which suggest that students need to be taught to be more strategically aware of their goals, and to be given the means to achieve these goals in writing. One example of this is influenced by the development of cognitive genre-based approaches to teaching academic reading and writing (Bruce, 2008). The organization of ideas within a paragraph is viewed as a sub-genre of the macro-level essay genre; hence the inclusion of tasks on paragraph development and on the integration of different rhetorical patterns within one piece of writing.

Flower et al. (1990) assert that recognizing and exploring the rhetorical problem is a teachable process, through the development of strategies for appropriate goals. Chamot & O'Malley (1994) argue that research has found that effective learning relates more to how strategies are used than to the overall number of strategies used (p. 7). The latter researchers suggest scaffolding techniques for learning these strategies, which they subdivide into *metacognitive strategies* (thinking about and evaluating one's learning process), *cognitive strategies* (interacting with material to be learnt), and *socio-affective strategies* (interacting with another person to assist learning). The fact that people write in different ways at different stages of their writing development (Bereiter & Scardamalia, 1987) reinforces the requirement for scaffolded activities. The practical implications are that one should: teach students how to use strategies to achieve their goals in writing; develop scaffolding techniques; familiarize students with a variety of task and genre types; and describe an explicit route through the teaching materials.

This combined approach, taking into account the process approach, the development of critical thinking in writing, the microskills of writing and the importance of genre, reflects the major emphasis many researchers place on the need for a balance between the processes of writing (creative, cognitive, communicative) and the demands made by the contexts in which writing takes place and by the purposes for which it takes place (Tribble, 1996; Grabe & Kaplan, 1996; Johns, 1993; Leeds, 1996). An implicit interpretation of this view can be seen in the reviewing, focusing and evaluating phases of the process model; it can be assumed that the writer applies judgement to carry out these processes in the context of his/her understanding of (and feedback on) the particular discourse conventions and social context of the assignment in question. Johns (1993) argues that there is 'a natural integration of process and product in academic writing' (p. 276).

The importance of the reader

Research findings have also recognized the strong role of the 'outside reader' when writers make decisions about their approach to a task; Raimes (1991) describes the reader as 'powerful'. The reader is the person who will read and judge the end product. One of the implications of this research is that consideration needs to be given to the impact of rhetorically specific wording – that is, analyzing the demands that the task makes upon the reader in terms of how he or she constructs a response. This involves consideration of language use and structural organization. Hence, in *EAS: Writing*, activities are included in which students carefully analyze the writing task, with the goal of raising students' awareness of these aspects of writing before they start to plan and to write.

It is valuable to refer back to the introduction as you work your way through the book with your class, in order to put an activity into the context of the approach. For example, after carrying out a peer-evaluation session, you could refer back to the section on critical thinking skills and ask students how they feel their critical thinking has developed after completing the peer evaluation.

Using *EAS: Writing*

Pair and group work

Many of the activities on this course require students to participate in a considerable amount of discussion with their classmates – for example, about how they think they should develop an essay structure, or for purposes of sharing ideas about content. The aim of these discussions and comparisons of answers is to heighten students' awareness of various issues: for example, that there is more than one way to approach a problem, that there is no single right answer, and that in carrying out discussion they develop their critical thinking ability. Although it might seem that, in what is stated to be a writing course, there is rather a lot of discussion; in fact, by verbalizing their thoughts, students can develop their writing strategies further. This needs to be explained *explicitly* to the students, some of whom may question why they are talking so much in a writing class.

The rate at which you complete the activities and work in the book will depend on the level and experience of your class. To some extent, this flexibility is built into the Teacher's Book, but you will also need to exercise your own judgement as to how long you need to spend on particular exercises. Some students will find certain tasks very challenging, but usually when encouraged to pursue them they will see the benefit, and their writing will improve.

Multiple drafting

An inevitable result of adopting the process approach is that students will often be working on the first draft of one essay while revising a previous essay so as to produce a third draft. You will soon get into a pattern of timing and organization, so that neither you nor the students are overwhelmed by the amount of work there is to be done.

Marking and giving feedback

Feedback plays an integral role in the teaching of academic writing, but effective evaluation and feedback require time and attention: 'It is a highly skilled teaching process' states Hamp-Lyons (2006). There are both text-level issues (e.g., content, organization, argument) and local-level issues (e.g., language, punctuation, spelling) to consider. Suggestions of a workable framework for feedback are made in this book. However, it is acknowledged that a range of feedback methods and strategies are useful, and it is expected that teachers will bring their own experiences to bear on such a framework. The research literature on feedback since 1985 is substantial, and a detailed discussion of this cannot be offered here. However, it is worth mentioning two relevant conclusions of certain research projects. Ferris's (2006) study on whether student writers are helped by error feedback found 'a strong relationship between teachers' error markings and successful student revisions on the subsequent drafts of their essays' (p. 97). Hyland and Hyland (2006) warn against giving feedback which contains a heavy informational load that can prevent students from understanding the key areas for improvement in their writing.

Below is an effective approach to marking students' second drafts and giving feedback. By going through these stages of feedback over the duration of the course, students will markedly improve their writing skills.

At the end of this introduction, a photocopiable feedback form is provided. You can use this for making comments on specific aspects of the writing task:

- task achievement, i.e., how the student has responded to the writing task, as stated in the assignment title
- organization, i.e., how effectively the student has organized his/her ideas
- language, i.e., appropriate use of vocabulary and grammar
- content, i.e., relevance of content and depth of coverage
- additional comments

The form allows a record of students' progress to be compiled, which can be kept in their portfolios. These forms complement the peer evaluation sheets that are located at the back of the Course Book.

Note: All photocopiable materials in this book are also available as downloadable files in the teacher's section of the *EAS* website, www.englishforacademicstudy.com.

Language feedback

It is recommended that you use symbols to identify language errors, which the students then correct themselves. An example error correction sheet, along with a key to the symbols, is provided in photocopiable form at the end of this introduction. You may prefer to negotiate alternative meaningful symbols with your own students, and adjust the sheet accordingly; for example, in the case of lower-level students, you might prefer to limit the number of symbols they use at the beginning.

You should give students a completed error correction sheet when you return the second draft of their essays. Individual students can then count up the number of errors you have marked in each category and write it on the sheet. Students should also be encouraged to write a comment about each category, such as, 'I'll especially check for VF next time,' or 'I'll check the grammar rule for this.'

Students should keep all their essays in a file, as a portfolio, along with the error correction sheet. This will enable them to check their own progress. Students will have a target: to reduce the number of errors in each category over the duration of the course. It is suggested that you collect the error correction sheet with the third draft of the student essay. This will give you a chance to check whether students are completing the sheet and also to let you make a copy for yourself.

One method of dealing with feedback on the language errors commonly displayed in student writing is to identify one sentence in each student's essay that contains a common error. You can type these out, possibly adding the error correction symbols, and give each student a copy for him/her to study and identify the errors. The identification stage can be done at home or in class, but it is useful to follow up with a pair discussion in class, followed by a plenary with examples on an OHT or other visual medium. You can then discuss different ways in which each sentence could be corrected, ending up with a satisfactory version for all to see.

This approach:

- develops students' ability to self-correct language errors
- fosters students' critical ability
- helps build students' confidence in their ability to be proficient editors of their own work and respond effectively to the use of symbols

It is very likely that you will need to do some remedial work on students' language. A summary of the stages in giving feedback is given below.

1. Collect students' second drafts, along with their plans and first drafts.

2. Draw students' attention to language errors by using symbols marked on their scripts.

3. Comment on other aspects, marking on the feedback sheet and on the essay script (photocopy the feedback sheet).

4. Give back essays and feedback sheets, along with an error correction sheet.

5. Ask students to look at your feedback and ask you any questions that might arise; ask them to complete their error correction sheet.

6. Ask students to write a third draft, revising and correcting in line with your comments.

7. Collect second and third drafts; give feedback on how much revision students have done and on improvements; correct any outstanding language errors.

Timed writing

There are three timed writing activities, which should be completed during the course. The first one, in Unit 4, is preceded by some activities that aim to raise students' awareness of the process they go through when writing under time pressure. A suggested marking scheme is provided on pages 50–52. Two further timed writing activities are provided on pages 53 and 54.

Developing referencing skills using the Source Book

EAS: Writing focuses on developing students' ability to write in a clear and concise academic style. Incorporating ideas from sources to support the ideas of the writer, and referencing these, is an important aspect of academic writing. Scaffolded tasks are included to develop students' awareness of these issues, along with their skills in incorporating sources into their writing, using paraphrases and quotations, and in acknowledging sources accurately.

Students do need to appreciate the importance of acknowledging sources and need to start to notice how this is carried out. Students should be made explicitly aware that omitting references to sources amounts to theft of intellectual property, and that there could be serious repercussions should this occur in a genuine piece of academic writing they submit as part of future studies.

Should you wish to focus on the development of basic academic writing skills in line with the objectives of *EAS: Writing*, you can prepare the students for future work on referencing in the following two ways:

a. Recognizing different styles of referencing

Encourage students to notice that different sources may be referenced in different ways. Exposure to different referencing styles, and general discussion comparing style, content and intended readership, is not only important in terms of study skills, but will also prepare students for referencing their own sources. The Source Book contains texts of various types from a range of sources, with different examples of internal referencing.

Note: In *EAS: Writing*, single quotation marks are generally used to indicate quoted text because this is the publisher's house style. However, the APA referencing system, which is explained in Unit 2, requires double quotation marks. More on the use of quotations is available in *EAS: Extended Writing & Research Skills*.

You may like to explain to your students that, throughout the world, many different referencing systems are in use. The APA and the Harvard (Author-Date) systems are frequently used. It is important for students to check with their departments as to what referencing system is required.

b. Evaluating sources

Students need to assess the currency of any text they use to fulfil their reading purpose, and also assess the credentials of texts' authors. In the Source Book, as much guidance as possible is provided for this purpose (see, for example, the bibliographical information), and there is ample opportunity to explore author credentials and text currency by going beyond this. Students need to take into consideration the source of any text they use and the original intended readership. This should be a general teaching point at some stage of the teaching of every unit. Students should consider the academic weight that certain texts may carry in comparison with others in the Source Book. Teachers should also draw students' attention to the fact that the materials incorporate a range of texts, the intention being to develop students' exposure to relatively dense and content-packed texts, in preparation for their future academic studies.

Other features

Unit summaries: These give students an opportunity to reflect on what they have done at the end of each unit. You may want students to complete the unit summaries in class or in their own time. If they complete them out of class, time should be found in class to discuss what the students have done.

Key writing skills: These are explained where it is felt that students need specific information on an area of writing. They usually appear at the end of a task, so that they can reflect on the skills, having completed the task.

Glossary: This contains a useful list of terms that students will need to know during the course.

Study tips: These provide additional information that students can use as a ready reference to a range of study issues related to the skill of writing.

Methodology notes: These appear in the Teacher's Book and give some ideas for alternative ways that you could use the material with your class.

Study skills: These are suggestions you may like to make to students that will aid them throughout the process of writing an academic essay.

Extension activities: These are activities that allow for further practice of a particular writing skill.

***Assessing my progress* form:** The appendix on pages 92–93 of the Course Book contains an *Assessing my progress* form for students to complete once they have finished the course. They should use it to assess the progress they have made on the course, by evaluating the essays they have written and deciding on their strengths and weaknesses.

References

Belcher, D., & Braine, G. (Eds.), (1995). *Academic writing in a second language*. Norwood: Ablex.

Bereiter, C., & Scardamalia, M. (1987). *The psychology of written composition*. Hillsdale, NJ: Erlbaum.

Bloor, M., & Bloor, T. (1986). *Languages for specific purposes: practice and theory*. Dublin: Centre for Language and Communication Studies, Trinity College.

Bruce, I. (2008). *Academic writing and genre: a systematic analysis*. London: Continuum.

Bruner, J. S. (1983). *Child's talk: Learning to use language*. Oxford: Oxford University Press.

Carson, E. J., & Leki, I. (Eds.), (1993). *Reading in the composition classroom*. Boston, MA: Heinle and Heinle.

Chamot, A., & O'Malley, J. (1994). *The CALLA handbook: Implementing the cognitive academic language learning approach.* Reading, MA: Addison-Wesley.

Etherington, S. (2008). Academic writing and the disciplines. In P. Friedrich (Ed.) *Teaching Academic Writing*. London: Continuum International Publishing Group Ltd.

Ferris, D. (2006). Does error feedback help student writers? New evidence on the short- and long-term effects of written error correction. In K. Hyland & F. Hyland (Eds.), *Feedback in Second Language Writing: Contexts and Issues*. Cambridge: Cambridge University Press.

Flower, L., Stein, V., Ackerman, J., Kantz, M. J., McCormick, K., & Peck, W. C. (1990). *Reading to write: Exploring a cognitive and social process*. Oxford: Oxford University Press.

The Framework for Higher Education Qualifications in England, Wales and Northern Ireland. (August 2008). Retrieved 2, May 2012 from http://www.qaa.ac.uk.

Friedrich, P. (2008). *Teaching Academic Writing*. London: Continuum International Publishing Group Ltd.

Grabe, W., & Kaplan, B. (1996). *Theory and practice of writing*. London: Longman.

Hamp-Lyons, L. (2006). Feedback in portfolio-based writing courses. In K. Hyland & F. Hyland (Eds.), *Feedback in Second Language Writing: Contexts and Issues*. Cambridge: Cambridge University Press.

Hyland, K. (2002). *Teaching and Researching Writing*. London: Longman.

Hyland, K., & Hyland, F. (2006). Interpersonal aspects of response: Constructing and interpreting teacher written feedback. In K. Hyland & F. Hyland (Eds.), *Feedback in Second Language Writing: Contexts and Issue*. Cambridge: Cambridge University Press.

Johns, A. (1993). Reading and writing tasks in English for Academic Purposes classes: Products, processes, and resources. In E. J. Carson & I. Leki (Eds.), *Reading in the composition classroom* (pp. 274–289). Boston, MA: Heinle and Heinle.

Johns, A. (1997). *Text, role and context: developing academic literacies*. Cambridge: Cambridge University Press.

Leeds, B. (Ed.), (1996). *Writing in a second language*. London: Longman.

Leki, I. (1995). *Academic writing: exploring processes and strategies*. New York: St. Martin's Press.

Raimes, A. (1991). Out of the woods: Emerging traditions in the teaching of English. *TESOL Quarterly, 25*, 407–430.

Richards, R. (1999). *An overview of the literature on EAP writing*. Unpublished manuscript.

Tribble, C. (1996). *Writing*. Oxford: Oxford University Press.

Zamel, V., & Spack, R. (1998). *Negotiating academic literacies: teaching and learning across languages and cultures*. Mahway, New Jersey; London: Lawrence Erlbaum Associates.

Routes through the materials

As stated before, *EAS: Writing* can either be used in combination with *EAS: Reading*, published in the same series, or as a stand-alone course. The books are designed for international students of English intending to pursue academic study in an English-speaking environment, whose IELTS level is between 5.0 and 7.5+. However, much of the material can be adapted for use with less proficient students studying an extended course.

One of the key principles underpinning the approach taken to academic reading is the idea that it should be purposeful; thus, writing provides a purpose for reading in an academic context. The type of information required to complete the writing task will determine the type of reading needed to extract the relevant information and ideas from the text. **Note:** Written focus tasks are indicated in many units of *EAS: Reading*.

On pages 14–15 are a number of suggested routes through the course material, depending on the length of the intended course and the number of probable teaching hours required to reach the minimum university entrance level. Each of the routes is based on two 90-minute lessons per week. Bear in mind that the amount of work given to students to be completed outside class time will vary, but inevitably a certain number of hours will be needed to complete written assignments. Students with a higher level of English-language proficiency are expected to cover the units more quickly than lower-level students.

Note: The allocation of time does not include time for reading the Source Book materials. It is suggested that such reading should take place outside the classroom.

Suggested route for 16-week course

Week	Contact hours	Unit
1	3	Unit 1 and Unit 2
2	3	Unit 2
3	3	Unit 2
4	3	Unit 3
5	3	Unit 3
6	3	Unit 4
7	3	Unit 4
8	3	Unit 4
9	3	Unit 5
10	3	Unit 5
11	3	Unit 6
12	3	Unit 6*
13	3	Unit 7
14	3	Unit 7*
15	3	Unit 8
16	3	Unit 8

*It is intended that students are encouraged to take more responsibility for independent study with Units 6 and 7.

Suggested route for 10-week course

Week	Contact hours	Unit
1	3	Unit 1
2	3	Unit 1
3	3	Unit 2
4	3	Unit 2
4	3	Unit 3
5	3	Unit 4
6	3	Unit 4
6	3	Unit 5
7	3	Unit 5
7	3	Unit 6
8	3	Unit 6
9	3	Unit 7
10	3	Unit 7

Suggested route for 8-week course

Week	Contact hours	Unit
1	3	Unit 1
2	3	Unit 2
3	3	Unit 2
4	3	Unit 3
5	3	Unit 4
6	3	Unit 4
7	3	Unit 6
8	3	Unit 6

Suggested route for 5-week course

Week	Contact hours	Unit
1	3	Unit 1
2	3	Unit 2
3	3	Unit 4
4	3	Unit 6
5	3	Unit 7

Feedback on writing tasks

Name:		Date:	
Task:		Teacher:	

Task achievement:

Language:

Additional comments:

Organization:

Content:

PHOTOCOPIABLE

Photocopiable handout

Error correction sheet

Text title:	

Error type		Number	Example or comment
WO	word order		
WF	word form		
VOC	vocabulary choice		
VF	verb form		
S/V	subject/verb agreement		
T	tense		
CL	clause construction		
PR	preposition		
AR	article		
C	noun is countable		
S/PL	singular or plural change needed		
AV	use active voice		
PV	use passive voice		
–	missing word or words		
R	redundant word(s)		
IR	irrelevant information		
INF	language too informal		
P	punctuation		
PARA	paragraph problem		
SP	spelling mistake		
?	meaning unclear		

PHOTOCOPIABLE

Introduction to academic writing

In this unit students will:

- think about the purpose and process of academic writing
- reflect on their own experiences and expectations of writing

Task 1   Thinking about academic writing

The questionnaire is designed to stimulate students to think about the purpose, process and mechanics of academic writing. It will also encourage them to think about their individual experience of academic writing. It should raise students' awareness of some of the critical thinking skills involved in writing in higher education institutions.

Some students may find it difficult to think analytically about these aspects and will need extra support. If you have a lower-level group, you can choose to omit some of the more challenging sections, and come back to them later in the course when students' awareness has developed further. Remind students that the aim of the questionnaire is to prompt them to think about the requirements of writing in an academic setting and there are *no right or wrong answers*.

Students should complete the questionnaire on their own, but monitor and check that they understand the questions. Some of the more difficult vocabulary items are defined using footnotes within the text. After working individually, students can then discuss their answers in groups; after that, they can offer the most interesting points of their discussion to the rest of the class as part of a plenary.

Questionnaire outline

1.1– 1.3, 1.7– 1.12   These questions focus on academic writing. You may want to explain that surveys carried out among academic departments in English-speaking universities suggest that in the academic writing of international students, *content*, *organization* and *vocabulary* are considered the most important aspects by subject tutors. Many tutors will tend to overlook minor errors in grammar as long as these do not seriously interfere with comprehension.

1.4– 1.6   These questions focus on the development of the critical thinking skills involved in writing, which students are expected to have or to develop during their time at university. This is based on research carried out at English-speaking higher education institutions.

Possible answers:

Questions 1.1–1.6
The answers on pages 19–20 are guidelines only; students should be encouraged to justify alternative suggestions and thus provoke discussion.

1.1   **What is academic writing? Tick (✔) one or more.**

- ☐ a mechanical exercise
- ☐ groups of grammatically correct sentences
- ☑ the clear expression of ideas, knowledge and information
- ☐ a form of self-expression
- ☐ a way of exploring, addressing and expressing academic issues
- ☐ a way of communicating results or information

1.2   **How important are these points for good academic writers? Tick (✔) _H_ for High importance, _M_ for Medium importance, _L_ for Low importance.**

H	M	L	
☑	☐	☐	reading a lot
☐	☑	☐	studying grammar
☐	☑	☐	studying vocabulary
☐	☐	☑	imitating other writers
☑	☐	☐	writing a lot
☑	☐	☐	inviting others to comment on your writing
☑	☐	☐	going back and thinking again about what you have written
☑	☐	☐	rewriting repeatedly until you are satisfied
☐	☑	☐	understanding the process of writing
☑	☐	☐	meeting the needs of your reader

With the final answer, emphasize the importance of considering who the intended reader is. Point out that a writer should always consider the following:

- Who will my reader be?
- What does my reader already know about the topic?
- What will my reader want to know?
- Why will my reader want to know this?

1.3   **How important are the following when writing academic texts? Tick (✔) _H_ for High importance, _M_ for Medium importance, _L_ for Low importance.**

H	M	L	
☐	☑	☐	grammatical correctness
☐	☑	☐	spelling and punctuation (using full stops and commas, etc.)
☑	☐	☐	an appropriate style
☑	☐	☐	overall organization
☐	☑	☐	vocabulary
☑	☐	☐	good ideas
☑	☐	☐	good use of sources (appropriate **citation**, bibliography)
☑	☐	☐	relevance of subject content
☑	☐	☐	response to the task

1.4 Which of the following can be used to support your ideas when writing academic texts?

- [ ] personal anecdotes*
- [✔] facts
- [✔] statistics
- [✔] examples
- [ ] the news
- [✔] information from books, articles, reports, the Internet
- [✔] analogies†
- [✔] the views and attitudes of others
- [✔] research data

*anecdote: a short, often amusing account of a person or an event
†analogy: a comparison of one or more things that have similar features

1.5 Which of the following contribute to successful academic writing?

- [✔] presenting information clearly and precisely
- [✔] analyzing questions and issues clearly and precisely
- [✔] distinguishing between relevant and irrelevant material
- [✔] recognizing key assumptions*
- [✔] identifying competing points of view
- [✔] demonstrating excellent reasoning and problem-solving abilities
- [✔] adopting a critical stance
- [✔] understanding the context for which you are writing

*assumption: a belief that something is true without having any real proof or evidence
†critical stance: a strong viewpoint on something after examining it carefully

1.6 How important are the following when persuading others that your argument is valid? Tick (✔) *H* for High importance, *M* for Medium importance, *L* for Low importance.

Note: You need to persuade people in the *academic community* such as your tutor and examiners.

H	M	L	
✔			analyzing questions
	✔		stating facts
✔			reasoning your argument logically from facts
✔			explaining key terms
✔			using language appropriate to a particular subject area
✔			using other points of view to strengthen your argument or research
✔			demonstrating the weaknesses of other people's arguments
✔			acknowledging the limitations of your own argument or research
✔			supporting your argument with examples
✔			frequently summarizing your argument
✔			referring to well-argued conclusions

There are a number of different ways of answering the remaining questions. Some possible answers are given below. You may also wish to make notes relating to your own ideas, particularly for questions 1.9–1.12, as these refer specifically to personal experiences with academic writing.

1.7   Should you always think of academic writing as communicating with another person? Why/why not?

There are various forms of academic writing that can involve different kinds of communication with a reader. Such communication is not always one-way. For example, replies to academic texts are written in the form of letters, articles and conference papers by people with opposing points of view. You could mention:

- published academic books
- articles published in academic journals
- papers given at academic conferences
- dissertations and unpublished monographs found in libraries
- essays given by students to tutors

The form of communication in each of these will be slightly different, for example, depending on the anticipated level of knowledge the reader is likely to have on the topic. It is therefore always important to consider who the intended reader will be and how you will need to adapt your writing and the content as a result.

1.8   What do you focus on when you are working on these areas of a writing task:

1. while you are writing your first draft
   - *how you can integrate what you have been reading with your own ideas*
   - *the best way to organize and develop your points within the essay*
   - *how to summarize your main ideas in a clear introduction and conclusion*

2. when you have finished your first draft
   - *what improvements can be made to the organization, content and language used in your first draft*
   - *whether your ideas are easy to follow*
   - *checking that you have backed up your ideas with evidence and examples*

3. before you hand in your final draft
   - *checking that you have made all the necessary changes*
   - *ensuring your points are referenced correctly*
   - *a final read-through and proofreading check*

1.9–1.12
Answers depend on students (according to their background).

2 Sustainable energy

In this unit students will:

- make decisions about what the essay is asking them to write about
- consider the most appropriate way to organize their ideas
- write an introduction to their essay
- decide what information in a text is useful to support their ideas
- incorporate information from a text into their writing
- acknowledge their sources accurately

As preparation for writing, students should read Texts 2a and 2b in the Source Book (pages 8–11, both entitled *Using waste, Swedish city cuts its fossil fuel use*). If you are not using *EAS: Reading*, the reading purpose should be to identify information relevant to the essay title:

How can alternative sources of energy be harnessed effectively?

In this case, the content of the texts should be discussed in plenary to check comprehension and to focus the students' thinking.

Task 1 | Microskills: Planning your writing

1.1   This is a good opportunity to raise students' awareness of the importance of analyzing essay questions (for both examinations and course assignments). Point out that this will help them understand what the examiners/lecturers require in the answer.

Answers:
- alternative sources of energy
- harnessed
- effectively

You may need to explain the verb *harness*.

1.2   Encourage the students to write down as many notes and ideas as they can, no matter how important they think they are at this stage. As this is the first essay in the book, the plenary stage of this brainstorming task is very important.

Encourage the students to consider the ways in which the essay can be developed, and the fact that the essay should not just answer the question by giving examples. The essay should provide:

- some background information about why there is consideration of the use of alternative energy (e.g., cost and depletion of fossil fuels, pollution)
- examples of use of these types of energy
- some evaluation of the effectiveness of the different forms of alternative energy

It may be useful to frame the plenary discussion within these three key areas. Encourage the students to add ideas that they have not already thought of themselves to their notes.

1.3   Not all students will be willing to work in pairs or groups at the beginning of the course. Make sure you encourage the students to see this as a useful part of the programme as they will work in this way throughout the course.

1.4/
1.5

Students need to be made aware of how important planning is, right from the start of the course. Emphasize that if students spend time planning carefully from the beginning, they can save a lot of time later.

Highlight the importance of considering who the reader will be to help them select which ideas and points to include in their essay. You may like to build up a profile of the intended reader for this particular essay on the board.

Some groups may find it useful to see a model of a good plan, with both paragraphing and the main ideas within paragraphs easily identifiable. One approach to producing such a plan is provided as a photocopiable handout, Appendix 2a, on page 32. You might like to project this onto a screen and build up paragraph topics with the students, or you could give each student a copy to be completed for their own essay. You could also elicit other possible ways of planning.

1.6

Although it is still early on in the course, students should be able to answer the five questions designed to evaluate each other's plan. However, you may need to run through the questions, prompting students on what to look for.

Remind students of the benefits of having another person look at their plans, i.e., if the plan is clear to another person, then the writer has successfully considered the logical organization and content of his/her essay. At this early stage in the course, you could consider asking students to work in groups of three so that two people work together to evaluate each plan.

1.7

Students reflect on the comments on their plans and make the necessary changes. Highlight that this may involve going back to the source texts and adding ideas where needed.

Writing the first draft

Students begin to write their essays at this stage (marked throughout the Course Book by a blue box). Remind the students that this course is based on a process-writing approach and they will be expected to improve their drafts as they receive further input during the unit, i.e., at this point, you will not expect too much in terms of academic structure.

Point out that each student will be expected to write between 400 and 600 words.

Task 2	Peer evaluation

2.1

Depending on the amount of progress made by your particular group, you will need to decide whether to undertake the peer evaluation before or after you cover the microskills sections on incorporating other sources into an essay and writing introductions in Tasks 3 and 4 respectively. The advantage of undertaking this evaluation afterwards is that students will be much more aware of what makes a good introduction, and will be fully able to evaluate a partner's work. However, it may also be useful to introduce the idea of peer evaluation at this earlier stage so they can start to develop the necessary skills.

2.2/
2.3

As this is the first peer evaluation session of the course, it is important for an atmosphere of cooperation to be established. Emphasize the positive aspects of evaluation and of constructive criticism, as well as the fact that the evaluator is making suggestions that the writer may or may not choose to implement. However, the writer also needs to understand that a reader's viewpoint is very valuable. The writer might know exactly what he/she is writing about, but may inadvertently omit the links that a reader needs in order to understand the direction or development of the writer's ideas.

It may be helpful to remind students of the importance of expressing views in a 'non-threatening' way, using suitable language. You could discuss with them the difference between the following two examples:

■ *You can't/shouldn't do/write that …*
■ *It might be easier for the reader to understand this idea if you added more information about …*

Guide students through the selection of suitable phrases for making polite suggestions provided on page 18 of the Course Book.

Methodology note: Dealing with a reluctance to give/receive peer feedback

Students can be resistant to the idea of peer evaluation, believing that only the teacher can comment on their work.

If students are made explicitly aware of the benefits of this stage in the writing process, the idea will become more acceptable and relevant to them. You may want to highlight the following points:

■ Peer evaluation trains students to be more critical of the written word, and this eventually enables them to evaluate their own essays from the reader's viewpoint more quickly and efficiently.
■ Peer evaluation contributes to the development of critical thinking skills.

Once the students start their academic course, you will not be with them. They will need to depend on themselves and on their friends for feedback before submitting assignments.

Peer evaluation sheets

For each essay the students write, there is a peer evaluation sheet with very specific questions that students should respond to. The main reason for this is that students are likely to find this stage difficult at first, and may not be able to focus and be critical about all aspects of writing.

The development of the skill of giving peer feedback is carefully staged, so that the students gradually build up their ability to evaluate writing. As well as referring to overall structure and general points, the questions will relate to the *microskills* that are being taught in the class. So, for example, in Unit 3 where you have been looking at paragraph leaders, the peer evaluation will include questions like 'Can you identify the paragraph leader in each paragraph?' You may find that some students want to modify the language in the essays they are peer-evaluating. To avoid *inappropriate* correction, you may want to tell them that you, as the language specialist, will look into language problems when you see the students' second drafts.

As you circulate and monitor the students, decide whether you want to intervene in the peer evaluation process and, if so, to what degree. During the early stages of the course, some students will need guidance from you, while others will only want confirmation on one or two points. It is important for students to build up their confidence in their ability to analyze the effectiveness of their peers' writing.

Methodology note: Organizing peer feedback

Experiment with organizing peer feedback within groups of three. This is particularly useful if you find some students are better at peer evaluation than others, or when there is some resistance.

Ideally, students in each pair or group should be of a mixed language background. Speakers of the same language tend to organize their writing in similar ways and to make similar language errors. However, it is not always possible to get this mix, and there may be other relevant factors, such as level and ability.

The first peer evaluation sheet requires students to consider the overall structure of an academic essay and the clarity of ideas presented. The questions anticipate remedial or revision work on what makes a good introduction and conclusion, and the importance of paragraphing. You will need to decide the degree to which you want to anticipate this, and how much discussion you want to encourage, according to the needs of your group.

The time given to peer evaluation can vary according to the level of the class. Initially, allow *at least* 45 minutes, as students need time to read the essay and then answer the questions. As the question sheets become more detailed, and the essays longer, an hour might be needed, even with a very good group.

It is useful to end the session in plenary, going round the class and asking each student what he/she is going to change in his/her individual draft. It can be efficient to restrict each student to mentioning only one change. The fact that students have some concrete changes to make helps to demonstrate the usefulness of the session.

Peer evaluation sheet: Unit 2

Task 1
Ask the students to read the questions on the peer evaluation sheet and ask for clarification.

Section 1.1: Introduction
a. The students should be able to identify whether the essay has an introduction.
b. You may want to suggest that the introduction should mention the 'key ideas' in the title and explain how the writer is going to approach the topic.
c. Students who are new to this process will have difficulty in making suggestions for improvement. You may want to prompt here, although they should find this easier once they have worked through Task 4 on writing introductions later in the unit.

Section 1.2: Paragraphing
a–b. You may want to remind students that each paragraph should contain a main idea, which is then developed in the paragraph. You may also want to discuss the benefits of having a logical order of ideas.

c. This question is asking students to decide whether there is enough detailed explanation of the ideas, or enough examples provided to illustrate the point.

Extension activity
Later activities and units will focus on exemplification and the development of ideas. However, if you feel the need to be more explicit about the development of ideas in a paragraph at this stage, you might build up an example on the board. For example, put up this sentence on the board:

Learning English is useful.

Then ask the students how they could develop the idea. Emphasize that if this idea is not developed, the reader will be asking him/herself questions like:

Why *is it useful?* or **How** *is it useful?* or **Who** *is it useful for?*

This should elicit answers similar to the following:

It is useful because a knowledge of English enables people to access more information. For example, scientists need to be able to read research articles and books written in English to keep up to date in their field. A knowledge of English is also useful for international communication, as it is the most widely spoken language.

Encourage students to ask the questions *How? Why? When? For whom?* about every statement they write. This should help them increase their awareness of the need to develop their ideas in their writing, as well as foster a critical approach to their studies.

Section 1.3: Incorporation of sources

At this stage, if students have done the microskills work, they should be able to identify any ideas taken from the texts and comment on the success of any paraphrasing and acknowledgements.

As this is essential academic practice, and a step towards avoidance of plagiarism, it is worth emphasizing that students should check that no parts of their partner's text have been copied word-for-word from the source texts, and that, in the second draft, changes are made to eliminate any copying.

Section 1.4: Conclusion

Some students may have no idea about what makes a suitable conclusion. You may want to explain briefly that, in the conclusion, the main ideas should be referred to, and that it could:

- be a summary
- draw conclusions
- look to the future

This anticipates a future teaching session on writing conclusions.

Section 1.5: Additional information

This question involves students assessing and evaluating the texts they have read with the purpose of identifying relevant information they can add to their essays. Some students may find this difficult, so it would be a good idea to have a plenary discussion on this and remind students of the importance of continually revising their drafts and including new ideas. They may like to think about whether they had included any ideas in their own draft which might be added to their partner's to improve it, and vice versa.

Task 2

Before they give each other feedback on the drafts, remind them of the phrases on Course Book page 18 and the importance of highlighting the strengths as well as the areas that can be improved.

Task 3

Students work individually to consider the feedback they have received and make more detailed notes on the changes they might make in their second draft. Remind them that it is up to them which comments they agree with and decide to act on, but they should be willing to consider different ways of constructing their essay.

Then ask the students to rewrite their draft in class or for homework, incorporating the improvements they have identified.

Task 3	Microskills: Incorporating other sources into an essay

3.1/ 3.2 Students could make decisions about appropriate parts of the texts to use for homework, and then share their ideas in class.

The experience of the city of Kristianstad provides a good example of how alternative energy can be harnessed, so students are likely to identify details of how they go about this. These could include: Text 2a, lines 18–35 (as in the Course Book Task 3.5), lines 49–59, lines 73–87 (for examples in the United States); Text 2b, lines 29–56, 72–91.

3.3 For some students, this may be the first time that they have had to think about how to use information from texts in their writing, and they may not know how to answer the question. It can be viewed as an awareness-raising question, which will lead to discussion of what is acceptable and not acceptable in UK academic writing, i.e., that chunks of text should not be copied verbatim.

3.4 Ex 3.4 and Ex 3.5 take students through the process of summarizing relevant information from a text. This can be a difficult skill to acquire, but it is an essential one that students should practise frequently. They should begin by reading through the green information panel on page 19. You could write up the labels *key ideas* and *secondary ideas or examples* and ask students which of the two ideas given go under each category.

Answers:
1. energy sources such as potato peels – key idea
2. the heat generated from waste products – secondary idea/example

3.5 After the students have read through the extract, go through Steps 1–5 together, highlighting the process they should go through to create a diagram of notes like the one shown on page 20.

3.6 This is Step 6 of the process. The students can work individually or in pairs to complete the summary text.

Answer:

Waste <u>products</u> have been successfully harnessed to provide heat, <u>electricity</u> and car fuel in Kristianstad, Sweden. Potato peels, used cooking oil and stale biscuits are some of the discarded products, which are <u>biologically</u> processed to produce a type of <u>methane</u> gas, that can either be <u>burned</u> to produce heat and electricity, or <u>refined</u> to produce car fuel. Thus, normal everyday waste can be an <u>effective</u> alternative energy source, and should be considered as a solution to diminishing fossil fuel supplies.

Students work in pairs and go through Steps 1–6 using another relevant extract from the texts. Where useful, students' work could be shared with the class by using an OHT or other visual medium.

Note: Although Text 2a refers to *cookies* as an example of a waste product, the example notes and summary use the British English word *biscuits* instead. It may be a good idea to point out this difference between American and British English to students during this activity.

Many students struggle with how to appropriately acknowledge the sources of the information that they use in their academic writing. It is important to emphasize the necessity of accurate referencing throughout the writing course.

You could start a discussion by asking the students what the word *plagiarism* means. This can involve verbatim copying of text or paraphrasing another writer's ideas without acknowledging the source.

Highlight the two ways in which students need to acknowledge their sources:

1. writing full references at the end of their essay
2. including in-text citations within the body of the essay

Go over the format of the reference shown in the Course Book on page 21. Point out the different pieces of information that are included. It is important to stress that the format of these references is different depending on the type of text that is being referenced and the system of referencing that is used. They will need to find out which particular system is used and the conventions of this when they begin their university course. However, the basic practice of referencing remains fundamental to academic writing, whichever system is adopted.

Highlight the use of in-text referencing or citing within the main body of their essay. This typically includes the family name of the author and the year of publication. Citations for direct quotations will also include a page number, but there will be further input in later units of this book. Students should not be overloaded at this stage. Introduce students to one way of acknowledging the author within the text by writing on the board (Rosenthal, 2010), i.e., (Surname, year of publication).

You may like to give the students a different article to look at to practise writing an end-of-essay and an in-text reference, using the example as a model.

Extension activity: Thesis statements

Copy the thesis statement sheet on page 33 onto an OHT (or other visual medium) and go through the points with your students.

The ideas are adapted from Reid, J. M., (1988). *The process of composition*. Englewood Cliffs, NJ: Prentice Hall.

Then ask your students to identify the controlling ideas in the following statements. Ask them how they think the rest of the essay will be developed.
1. In South Africa, the AIDS epidemic is beyond human control.
2. Darwin's discovery of evolution has caused much controversy.
3. There are many reasons why international students decide to go abroad to study.

Ask your students to continue each statement with a sentence beginning: 'This essay will ...'

Students will get further practice of writing thesis statements in Ex 4.6.

Note: This may seem slightly prescriptive, but it has been shown that students find it useful at the beginning to adopt a formulaic approach, which they can break away from later when they have acquired a greater awareness of the requirements of academic writing.

| Task 4 | Microskills: Writing introductions |

4.1 This is a quick brainstorming activity to elicit students' prior knowledge. Put students in pairs or groups to discuss their ideas, and stress that it is also important to say why they have chosen these points.

Have a plenary discussion and write students' ideas on the board so the ideas are visible to students.

4.2 Using the points on the board and what they have heard during the plenary for the previous task, the students write their answers to the questions about writing introductions either individually or in pairs.

Stress that throughout the course, students will be developing their awareness of what makes a good introduction. However, point out that it is a good idea at the beginning to have a structure to follow.

Possible answers:
1. It introduces the topic and sets the context to orientate the reader. It usually outlines the main areas to be discussed during the essay.
2. A general statement about the topic, general information about the particular aspect of the subject to be covered in this essay, a brief outline of the main areas to be discussed and a statement of the writer's opinion or viewpoint on the topic.
3. Yes. Without an introduction, the reader will not know what is to be covered in the rest of the essay and will find it difficult to navigate through the ideas discussed.

4.3　In doing this exercise, students should begin to think of a general-to-specific pattern of organization for an introduction. Ask them to compare their order with another student before moving on to Ex 4.4.

4.4　You may like to briefly talk through the four different functions in the box to check that they understand what these mean before they assign them to the sentences in the table.

Answers (Ex 4.3/4.4):

Order	Sentence	Function
1	c	a <u>background statement about the topic</u>
2	a	<u>more specific information on the topic</u>
3	b	a statement of the <u>organizational framework</u>, which narrows the topic from general information to a specific viewpoint and states the controlling ideas of the essay and the intention of the writer
4	d	a statement of the <u>writer's viewpoint (stance)</u>; the reader would expect the writer to argue as to why developing educational opportunities is the most successful approach to relieving poverty

It is worth emphasizing to the students that one of the main aims in academic writing at English-speaking universities is for a writer to present his/her argument (viewpoint/stance) on an issue. Often this involves answering the questions *Why?* and *How?* You can refer students back to Unit 1, Ex 1.6.

Note: The writer's viewpoint or stance is also known as the *thesis statement*. At this point, it would be a good idea to refer students to the photocopiable handout, Appendix 2b, on page 33.

4.5　Give students time to look at these introductions individually. Then put them in pairs or groups to discuss their ideas. Highlight that the question these writers are answering is *not* the same as the one they have been focusing on for their own drafts.

Have a plenary to emphasize any useful and interesting points. There is no definite and specific answer to this exercise, as it involves evaluating introductions. However, the possible answers below may be useful (do not worry about language errors at this point).

Possible answers:
Introduction 1: This introduction contains a good example of the general-to-specific pattern: from alternative energy programmes in general in various countries, to the solar energy programme in a single country, Saudi Arabia. This introduction is very clear, but a little repetitive in places. However, the question requires a more general discussion of the most viable alternative energy sources, so the writer needs to take special care to explain to the reader why he/she is focusing on a single source in a single country.

Introduction 2: This is fairly successful; again, the writer needs to justify focusing their discussion on the situation in one particular region.

Introduction 3: This introduction has a rather rambling first sentence, with some instances of informal usage and of overgeneralizations (such as the use of *everybody*), and one irrelevant sentence (*China is a large country, so the possibility is good*). Another problem is that the reader is left 'hanging' at the end, wondering what *the related factors* are.

Thus, all in all, this introduction is not very successful, even though the overall message is conveyed. However, with revisions it would be acceptable.

Note: This may be an appropriate point at which to say something about formal style. Ask students if they think the style is appropriate in this introduction. They should come up with *Everybody* as inappropriate here. You could then discuss alternative expressions. Tell them that, traditionally, the use of *we* and *I* is not acceptable in academic writing either; however, it is often used in science and scientific journals when writing up experiments, and increasingly in subjects such as sociology or art history, where a personal response is asked for.

Introduction 4: This is a successful introduction, flowing from the general to the specific. Elicit an alternative word or phrase for *big* in the first sentence (e.g., *most significant*). Ask the students why you are suggesting making this change. You may like to use this opportunity to have a short discussion about how some words can sound more academic or formal in tone than others and therefore are more appropriate in this context.

Introduction 5: This requires some revision. Elicit possible ideas. Students should pick up on the inappropriateness of stating the first sentence as a question. The introduction does not flow well – it 'jumps' from one sentence to another because the links between ideas are not explicit. It is also slightly repetitive.

Extension activity

You could ask the students to rewrite Introduction 5 from the Course Book as a bridging task to the next exercise, if you feel they could benefit from this.

Possible answer:

There are many potential alternative energy sources. The value of these depends to a large extent on the country they need to serve; for example, the country's natural resources, the potential market and research systems and facilities already available. In Japan, there is much interest in alternative energy and many people have spent time researching the various options. This essay discusses the ways that alternative energy sources could be developed in Japan and discusses which one could be the most viable.

Note: The five introductions are versions of authentic student material – that is, they have been edited, so grammatical mistakes have been corrected and other changes made where considered appropriate.

4.6   Emphasize to the students that they do not need to write the whole essay. If you feel your students are not ready to write individually, they could do the first introduction in pairs, then project their introductions on an OHT (or other visual medium) for the class to evaluate.

4.7   Students should now have the confidence to revise the introductions of their first essay.

Unit summary

You may want the students to complete the unit summaries in class or in their own time. If they complete them outside of class, make sure you get some feedback during class time. This is particularly important for Ex 3. Depending on your group, you may wish to set up some of the tasks, either to clarify what to do, or to help get students thinking about the topics.

Some of the exercises can be done individually and others are best done in pairs or groups. When working outside the classroom, encourage students to find the time to meet with others and complete any pair or group activities.

1 This activity provides scaffolding for Ex 2.

Answers:

a. brainstorming
b. organizing ideas
c. adopting a critical stance
d. drafting
e. peer feedback

2 You may want to highlight that the form of some of the verbs from Ex 1 will need to change and they may also want to add some of their own ideas.

Possible answers:

a. When you are given a writing task, it is important to start by <u>reading the question carefully and brainstorming ideas</u>.
b. When you write the first draft, you should <u>organize your ideas first, and remember to adopt a critical stance. Remember to include an introduction and to acknowledge the sources of the information you include</u>.
c. Before you hand in your final draft, <u>try to get some peer feedback and continue to edit and redraft your work until you are happy with it</u>.

3 Encourage your students to allocate a particular notebook or part of a notebook as a diary of their progress. They may want to note down the following:

- a summary of what they have learnt during the unit
- things they have found easy and things they have found more difficult
- any particular action they want to remember to take during future writing activities (e.g., *don't forget to brainstorm and organize ideas first before starting to write* or *don't forget to acknowledge sources of information*)

Title: _____

Introduction

Thesis statement (also known as the writer's viewpoint or stance):

_____

Paragraph 1

Main idea: _____

Supporting idea 1: _____

Examples: _____

Supporting idea 2: _____

Examples: _____

Supporting idea 3: _____

Examples: _____

Paragraph 2

Main idea: _____

Supporting idea 1: _____

Examples: _____

Supporting idea 2: _____

Examples: _____

Supporting idea 3: _____

Examples: _____

Paragraph 3

_____

_____

Conclusion

_____

_____

_____

PHOTOCOPIABLE

Appendix 2b

Thesis statements

1. The thesis statement is probably the strongest statement in the essay.

2. The thesis statement will probably come at the beginning of the essay, usually at the end of the introductory paragraph.

3. A statement of fact, e.g., *Britain has three major political parties*, does not make a good thesis statement, as it does not provide the opportunity for extensive further development.

4. A question, e.g., *What is the main aim of academic study?* is not a good way to express the thesis. However, the answer to the question is the thesis: *The main aim of academic study is to develop an enquiring mind.*

5. The thesis statement will contain controlling ideas that will be further developed in the paragraphs of the main body of the essay.

6. The thesis statement will be specific.

Source: Adapted from Reid, J. M. (1988). *The process of composition*. Englewood Cliffs, NJ: Prentice Hall.

PHOTOCOPIABLE

3 The business of science

In this unit students will:

- make decisions about what the essay title is asking them to write about
- consider the most appropriate way to organize their ideas
- practise incorporating and referencing sources
- practise writing paragraph leaders

This unit will prepare the students to write an essay on the following topic:
Over the past 20 years, commercial influences on scientific research have become increasingly detrimental. Discuss.

This unit deals with a number of skills, in varying degrees of detail. Some of them will complement other academic skills work, e.g., summarizing information from a text and using this to support ideas, citing correctly, commenting on ideas; others will be recycled in later units. Higher-level groups should be able to deal with all of them. Lower-level groups will need to go into more depth in some skills compared with others, as indicated in the teacher's notes associated with each exercise.

Before beginning this unit, you may like to ask the students to briefly summarize the key points they learnt in Unit 2, perhaps drawing on the reflective notes they made at the end of the last task.

Task 1 | Microskills: Generating ideas

1.1   Give students between three and five minutes to do this task. It gives further practice in analyzing essay titles.

Answers:
1. ■ commercial influences
   ■ scientific research
   ■ detrimental
   ■ discuss

The students may not consider *discuss* to be one of the key words. If necessary, explain that an essay title can be divided into two parts:
- the words that refer to the subject or content of the essay
- the words that tell you what to do, e.g., *discuss*, *examine*

They will further explore the types of words in the second category in Unit 4. For now, they should understand that it is important to look out for these kinds of words.

1.2   Remind students that this should be a flow of all ideas connected with the topic, and the ideas do not have to be organized.

1.3   Place students into groups of three. The aim of this task is to stimulate students to process further their ideas about the demands of the title and to think about the direction of the essay.

1.4/   The aim of these tasks is to help students understand the demands of the title in a more
1.5   explicit way. As students have already brainstormed and discussed the topic, it should be easier for them to make a decision.

Answer:

The most appropriate answer is 4. However, it may be worth looking at the differences between descriptions 2 and 4.

Description 2 asserts that the commercial interests must be considered either damaging or enriching. However, the wording of the essay title suggests that the degree to which they are detrimental has changed over the years (*increasingly*) and, therefore, taking such a fixed stance may not be suitable.

The main point is that this is not a purely descriptive essay, but an essay that requires a discursive approach and an evaluation of the varying impacts of commercial influences, with an argument to the effect that some are more negative than others.

The word *discuss* should indicate that students are required to identify the various commercial influences and evaluate their impact, with a view to agreeing or disagreeing with the statement given in the title.

1.6 This task introduces the idea that there are different rhetorical patterns in writing and some may be more suitable than others for a particular topic. Weaker students may find this concept difficult, so you may want to move quickly on to the pair or group discussion.

The pattern can depend on the emphasis demanded by the essay title. For example, here the first section of the essay might discuss the different commercial influences on scientific research, then the extent of the influences, a discussion of the impacts, and the degree to which they are detrimental or not.

Elicit ideas and write them on the board. As this is a discursive essay, the better students would be expected to come up with something like:

- some background to how and why commerce interacts with scientific research
- a statement of the number and the labels of the different influences
- a paragraph or two on each one, which explain how the influence occurs, with some examples
- an evaluation of the theories/influences, considering both the positive and negative impacts

You may want to elicit from the students what might be an appropriate order. If they agree with the statement, then they may choose to focus on how and why the influences have become detrimental, followed by a discussion of counter-arguments that those with the opposite view might have (e.g., no research at all would be possible without commercial backing), while rebutting them.

This will also provide scaffolding for weaker students. However, point out that there is never only one way of approaching an essay title, and that different approaches will be looked at during the course. Students will then be in a position to make evaluative decisions as to the most effective approach to take towards their writing.

Note: If students are having difficulty coping with the whole essay, they can work at paragraph level rather than whole-essay level. Having decided what would be suitable topics for their paragraphs, students can work on one paragraph at a time in a more gradual way, building up their skills for developing an idea in a paragraph.

1.7 This reading task aims to develop the students' skills in using information from texts to develop their ideas.

Ask students to refer to Text 3a *Stop selling out science to commerce* and Text 3b *Is business bad for science?* (If you are using *EAS: Reading*, students will have read them already) in the Source Book (pages 12–16), then to identify information they think will be useful to answer the essay question. Encourage them to discuss their ideas in pairs or small groups, adding to the ideas brainstormed in Ex 1.2.

After students have discussed this in pairs, you may feel you need a plenary in order to share viewpoints. One way to do this would be to put the text on the screen and mark the relevant parts; the weaker students could then mark their own texts.

| Task 2 | Organizing ideas in your plan |

2.1 The stages here should be familiar to the students from Unit 1. Remind students of the value of planning their writing carefully. If they have most of their ideas down on paper in an appropriate order, and an indication of how their ideas will be supported and developed, it makes the writing of their essays more efficient.

Encourage students to use a sheet of A4 paper so that it is easier for them to add ideas and annotate their notes. It may be useful for some groups to see a model of a good plan, if you feel they are struggling with this task.

You could also refer back to Ex 1.6, which they could expand on to create their own, more detailed plan, adding a conclusion, e.g., a statement of whether they think the overall effect is increasingly detrimental or not, as stated in the essay question.

2.2 Read through the questions as a whole class before asking students to evaluate their partner's or another pair's plan.

2.3 Remind students that if someone else cannot understand their plan and has to ask a lot of questions, then the plan needs revising. Encourage students to make appropriate changes.

| Task 3 | Microskills: Incorporating and referencing your sources |

This section builds on the work done in Unit 2 on incorporating information from source texts appropriately. Here, students are guided to add their own comments to show their critical engagement with the subject matter, and integrate the information into their own argument.

3.1 Ask the students to read the extract from Text 3a and complete the notes in pairs, before sharing their ideas as a whole class.

Answers:

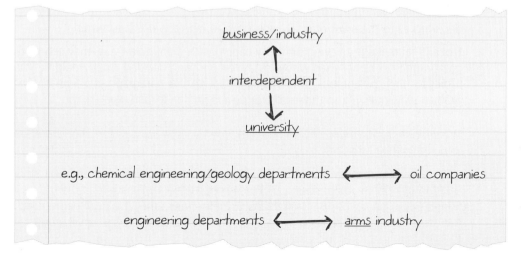

> **Study skills: Highlighting different forms of note-taking**
> It might be a good idea to point out that many of the examples of notes that are included in the Course Book are done in diagram form, rather than linearly. You could ask your students to experiment with these different note-taking methods. If they seem reluctant to do this, explain that you want to help them find the method of note-taking that works best for them, and this process involves trying out several different approaches. They may be surprised about which one they find the most effective.

3.2   The students summarize the information from the diagram in their own words. Again, they can do this in pairs if you feel that your group would be more productive working collaboratively.

3.3   The aim of this task is to encourage the students to check that they have not (inadvertently) duplicated exact sentences from the source text. You may want to elicit again why this is important.

Project or write the sentence below on an OHT (or other visual medium) and ask students to compare what they have written.

The marked increase in commercial financing of university departments, as with the oil industry's support for chemical engineering and geology, has led to diminished autonomy among academic staff.

3.4   Students will need to refer to the source texts to get the information they need to write these references. They should also look back at the notes on page 21 of their Course Books.

Answers:
a. Parkinson, S., & Langley, C. (2009). Stop selling out science to commerce. *New Scientist, 204*(2733), 32–33.
b. (Parkinson & Langley, 2009)

3.5   The aim of this and the following exercise is to take students onto the next stage of integrating others' ideas into their own writing, and also commenting on the ideas, which reflects a higher level of critical thinking.

Remind students that *comments* refers to a writer giving their own opinion or drawing on their own experience in response to something that they have read.

Answers:
The marked increase in commercial financing of university departments, as with the oil industry's support for chemical engineering and geology, has led to diminished autonomy among staff (Parkinson & Langley, 2009). It seems that academic researchers are obliged to research areas dictated by the industry concerned – areas which may be different from a researcher's particular interests. Of greater concern perhaps is the example that many engineering departments are funded by the arms industry. Thus, not only are university departments becoming more dependent on industry for funding, with restrictions on the type of research, but a number of departments receive funding from industries that could be seen as ethically unsound.

After students have compared answers, elicit answers and the reasons why they can be perceived as comments. Elicit signals such as *It seems that …, Of greater concern …*

By doing this, the writer has used the text to strengthen his argument about the detrimental effects on scientific research of commercial backing.

Explore the idea that it is good to have a concluding sentence in a paragraph, and *thus* is a useful signal for doing this. Concluding sentences will be dealt with in Unit 5.

The writer has emphasized the example of funding by the arms industry as the most extreme case of funding, and, by implication, one which conflicts with many of the ethics promoted by higher education.

3.6   Ensure that students follow all the steps outlined in Unit 2, Task 3, and Unit 3, Task 3.

Possible answers:
Research that leads to positive outcomes for society, especially for the poor and the hungry, is increasingly overlooked by funding bodies in preference for research that leads to a high level of profit. Genetics is a prime example of this selective funding within the field of agricultural science (Parkinson & Langley, 2009).

Many students will continue to need further practice in putting information from the text that they want to use for their essay into their own words. For many of them, it will be the first time they have met this idea.

You may like to do the Extension activity outlined below at this point to show students the different ways that they can refer to sources within their essay.

Extension activity: Other ways to express in-text referencing
Elicit and write on the board ways in which students can introduce ideas from other texts to support their writing. These might include:

- *As Ho and Saunders (2001) point out/pointed out, ...*
- *According to Parkinson and Langley (2009), ...*
- *Research carried out by Ho and Saunders (2001) shows/suggests that ...*
- *Ho and Saunders (2001) argue/argued that ...*
- *Ho and Saunders (2001) have drawn attention to the fact that ...*
- *In an article by Parkinson and Langley (2009), ...*
- *A study by Parkinson and Langley (2009) ....*
- *Ho and Saunders (2001) indicate/indicated that ...*
- *Parkinson and Langley (2009) claim/claimed that ...*
- *Ho and Saunders (2001) have expressed a similar view ...*

These in-text referencing ideas are also available as a photocopiable handout, Appendix 3a, on page 43.

Give the students some time to read through the source texts again and encourage them to add to their notes and revise their plan accordingly.

3.7   **Writing the first draft**
Students write the first draft of their essay. As in Unit 2, they should aim for between 400 and 600 words.

Remind them that you will expect to see a clear introduction and acknowledgements of their sources.

3.8   You should cover Task 4 before students complete their first draft and the peer evaluation sheet. Students should exchange their first drafts with another student before working through the peer evaluation sheet.

> **Peer evaluation sheet: Unit 3**
> Go through the sections of the peer evaluation sheet for this unit with the class. The sections of this peer evaluation sheet are similar to, but not the same as, the evaluation sheet from Unit 2.
>
> Remind the students again of the importance of looking for strengths as well as aspects that can be improved.

Task 1

Section 1.1: Introduction

a. The students should be able to indicate whether the introduction follows the pattern of moving from general to specific.

b. Students should be able to decide whether the writer has included a statement that shows how far they agree or disagree with the title of the essay.

c. If the students have worked through the exercises on writing introductions in the previous unit, they should be in a good position to give each other some more general feedback on their introductions. Refer the students back to these sections of the course materials as needed. If necessary, you could give them a short list of things they might want to look out for, including the inclusion of a thesis statement, explaining what they will cover within the rest of the essay, and beginning with a general statement about the topic (related to 1.1a above).

Section 1.2: Paragraphing

a.–b. You might like to remind students that there should be a logical flow of ideas through each paragraph, highlighting that each one should only focus on one main point.

c.–d. Paragraph leaders are covered in the next section of this unit. Students should be able to identify them at this stage.

e.–f. The important thing here is that the reader can understand and follow the points being made. If they can't, then the writer will need to redraft the relevant sections to make their ideas clearer.

g. Highlight that students should not include unnecessary or irrelevant information. Not all of the information given in the source texts will be relevant to this particular essay question, so it is important that they have been selective.

Section 1.3: Argument

Although students have not been taught explicitly about developing an argument, this is an opportunity to raise awareness about how the writer can weave his/her argument into their writing, and how writers need to convince the reader about their viewpoint by developing and referring to this throughout the essay.

a. Students should be able to recognize the writer's viewpoint, and whether this is maintained throughout the essay.

b. Students should be able to comment on the amount of evidence supporting the writer's argument.

c. This may be difficult for students to assess without having done some work on how to integrate opposing viewpoints.

d. Students should be able to answer this question.

Section 1.4: Incorporation of sources

a.–b. Remind students of the work they did on using ideas from the source texts and combining them with their own comments. They should check that the essay they are reading is *discursive* and not just *descriptive*.

Section 1.5: Conclusion

Conclusions will be covered in more depth in Unit 5, but for now, students should be able to consider whether they feel the conclusion summarizes the main points made in the body of the essay.

Tasks 2–3

Students should be familiar with these processes from Unit 2. You may also like to encourage the students to give each other feedback on how they gave the feedback. Did they point out positive aspects of the work as well as weaknesses? Did they use suitable language? Were their comments fair and accurate?

The *paragraph leader* is the first sentence in a paragraph, and can have a number of functions to make writing cohesive. The most common function of a paragraph leader used early in a writer's development can be likened to the more common label *topic sentence*. In this way, paragraph leaders can introduce the main idea of a paragraph.

4.1 The aim of this first task is to identify the important ideas in the examples of paragraph leaders taken from the source texts.

Answers:

a. Over the past two decades, <u>government policy</u> in the US, UK and elsewhere <u>has fundamentally altered the academic landscape in a drive for profit</u>. (Section 1, lines 17–19, page 12)

b. <u>Research is</u> also <u>undermined by misleading messages</u> put out by <u>industry-funded lobby groups.</u> (Section 2, lines 45–46, page 13)

c. Another <u>cornerstone</u> of science that is <u>being eroded</u> is <u>the freedom to set the public research agenda</u> so that it <u>serves the public interest</u>. (Section 3, lines 56–58, page 13).

4.2 The aim of this task is to raise further awareness, through discussion, of how to identify key ideas in a sentence, and how a good writer can help his/her readers by guiding them as to what comes next in the text. Higher-level students should reach agreement quite quickly, whereas lower-level students will need more time.

In each case, we would expect that the next sentences would further develop the point made, with examples and facts to illustrate it. Students will confirm their ideas in the next task, so there is no need to input detailed answers here.

4.3 Ask students to read the paragraphs following these sentences in the text (3a) and follow the instructions for a–c.

Answers:
Paragraph 1: (Section 1, lines 17–32, page 12) This paragraph develops the point that increased commercial links between universities and business leads to a lack of independence, and gives examples. The first sentence indicates this content.

Paragraph 2: (Section 2, lines 45–55, page 13) This paragraph develops the idea that some industries publicly question academic research. Again, this is signalled in the first sentence.

Paragraph 3: (Section 3, lines 56–74, page 13) This paragraph develops the idea that research focuses on areas that will lead to short-term profit rather than long-term benefits to society, which is again signalled in the first sentence.

4.4 Discuss the short paragraph about paragraph leaders (*Key writing skills: Paragraph leaders*).

As well as often indicating the topic of the paragraph, the paragraph leader acts as a cohesive device, linking the ideas of the essay with the title and with previous and subsequent ideas.

Stress the importance of writers helping their readers as much as possible, and that having a clear paragraph leader in each paragraph that signals the topic of the paragraph is one way of doing this.

Extension activity: Other forms of paragraph leaders
In this task, we have focused on the idea of paragraph leaders as topic sentences. However, if you are working with a higher-level class, you may like to discuss how paragraph leaders

can take more than one form. As well as a topic sentence that anticipates the main ideas of the paragraph, they can be:

- a statistic or fact that stimulates discussion about its truth and the evidence
- a quotation from a source that stimulates discussion

4.5   This task (and Ex 4.6) gives the students practice in deciding what makes a suitable paragraph leader.

Ask students to discuss their answers in small groups. The aim of this discussion is for students to clarify their ideas and reach agreement. Encourage students to explain the reason for their choice and say why they did not choose another option. This further develops their critical thinking.

Answers:

1. This sentence is not ideal as it only indicates a paragraph about how useful e-mail is in the office.

2. Again, this is not the best answer as it indicates a paragraph about only one use of e-mail (efficient communication with colleagues abroad).

3. Sentence 3 is the correct answer, as it indicates a discussion of the many uses of e-mail and does not narrow the discussion to a single point, as in the other two sentences.

4.6   Go through the same process with the sentences as in Ex 4.5.

Answers:

1. Sentence 1 indicates a paragraph about the reasons why studying in Britain is useful, but does not focus on the benefits to students in particular.

2. This is the correct answer, as it indicates a paragraph about the benefits to students of studying in Britain.

3. This sentence indicates a paragraph about why students prefer to study in Britain, which is not the focus of the question asked.

4.7   This task gives students practice in writing paragraph leaders. Ask the students to read the paragraphs and write suitable paragraph leaders.

Possible answers:

1. A knowledge of English has significant benefits in many working environments.

2. To solve the increasing traffic problem, a number of options need to be evaluated in order to establish how viable each of them is.

Writing paragraph leaders

Students should now have the confidence to include paragraph leaders in their essay for this unit. While they are making changes to their first drafts, they should be encouraged to revise their paragraphs in the light of the above activities.

Unit summary

1 Although much of this table is easy to complete, the students will nevertheless have to think carefully about some aspects. Encourage them to see this as an opportunity to reflect on what they have done and prepare for Ex 2.

Answers:

Skill	Task/exercise
Deciding what the essay is asking you to write	Task 1 (Ex 1.1–1.5)
Deciding the most appropriate way of organizing your ideas	Task 1 (Ex 1.6), Task 2
Deciding what information in a text is useful to support your ideas	Task 1 (Ex 1.7), Task 3 (Ex 3.1)
Incorporating that information in your writing	Task 3 (Ex 3.2–3.7)
Effectively introducing your reader to the main idea in each paragraph	Task 4

2 **Answers:**
a. key words
b. relevant
c. Discuss
d. develop; academic evidence
e. Group; related ideas
f. general statements
g. plan; first draft
h. paragraph leader

Appendix 3a

Other ways to express in-text referencing

As Ho and Saunders (2001) point out/pointed out, …

According to Parkinson and Langley (2009), …

Research carried out by Ho and Saunders (2001) shows/suggests that …

Ho and Saunders (2001) argue/argued that …

Ho and Saunders (2001) have drawn attention to the fact that …

In an article by Parkinson and Langley (2009), …

A study by Parkinson and Langley (2009) …

Ho and Saunders (2001) indicate/indicated that …

Parkinson and Langley (2009) claim/claimed that …

Ho and Saunders (2001) have expressed a similar view …

PHOTOCOPIABLE

4 Telemedicine

In this unit students will:

- understand the differences between writing an essay in an examination and writing a course assignment
- learn how to analyze the essay question quickly
- make decisions about the most appropriate way to organize their ideas
- complete an essay within a time limit

This unit will prepare the students to write a timed essay on the following topic:

As technology continues to improve, the range of potential uses for telemedicine will increase. Telemedicine will offer more beneficial applications in preventing rather than curing disease. Discuss.

The text that students will refer to in the Source Book, Text 4c, is preceded by two texts which are only used in the *EAS: Reading* course. Hence, Texts 4a and 4b are not mentioned in this book.

Task 1 | Writing in examinations

1.1   The aim of this task is to encourage students to think about the process they go through in answering examination questions.

Encourage the students to discuss their ideas together. You may or may not want to do a plenary discussion at this point, as the answers to these questions are contained within the rest of the unit. It might be an idea to return to these questions at the end of it and ask the students if they have anything to add to the notes they made.

Possible answers:

1. Read the question and underline the key words. Decide what the question is asking you to do.

2. Brainstorm ideas and think about which ones are relevant to the question.

3. Write out a plan including, if possible, paragraph leaders for each section. Then use this to write the essay.

1.2   When students have discussed among themselves, elicit ideas and discuss the differences.

Again, you may or may not wish to input a lot of information at this stage. It might be most useful to make a note of the points the students make and identify where there seem to be gaps in their knowledge or thinking.

Possible answers:
When students write an examination essay:

- they are writing within a specific time limit
- there is not time to write more than one draft
- the pressure of the exam can mean that they find it more difficult to write
- they don't get help from peers or teachers

1.3   The aim of this task is to consolidate students' understanding that writing in examinations is still a process, but is a shorter one than normal essay assignments.

Answers:

Stage in the process	Writing in examinations	Course assignments
1. Analyzing the title	✔	✔
2. Brainstorming ideas	✔	✔
3. Organizing your ideas/plan	✔	✔
4. Self-evaluation	✔	✔
5. Peer evaluation		✔
6. Writing a first draft		✔
7. Revising your draft	✔	✔
8. Writing a second draft		✔
9. Teacher evaluation/ feedback		✔
10. Evaluation of teacher feedback		✔
11. Revising your second draft		✔
12. Writing a third draft		✔
13. Writing a final draft		✔

Key writing skills: Stages in examination writing

Emphasize to students the importance of planning their time when writing an essay in an exam. Before they look at the breakdown in the table on page 35, you could ask the students how they would divide their time if they were given, for example, 45 minutes to write a 600-word essay. Discuss the need to allocate time for reading the question, brainstorming and planning, writing and reading through/editing.

Ask them to compare the time they have allocated to the suggestions on page 35.

Task 2	**Key words in examination questions**

2.1   This activity focuses on the key words that are used in examination and essay questions in general to indicate how the student is expected to engage with the information given. Understanding these is of fundamental importance and this should be emphasized to the students.

You may prefer to work through the questions section by section, depending on the level of your group. Some students may find matching the words very challenging as some of them have quite similar meanings.

Consider allowing the students to use monolingual dictionaries to help them identify the definitions.

Answers:

1. describe	6. discuss	11. account (of/for)	16. illustrate
2. define	7. analyze	12. consider	17. identify
3. summarize	8. compare	13. explain (why/how)	18. support
4. outline	9. contrast	14. prove	19. apply (to)
5. state	10. evaluate	15. comment (on)	20. relate

Task 3	**Interpreting example examination questions**

3.1/ 3.2

This task revisits the skill, already practised in previous units, of analyzing essay questions. You may wish to look at only three or four of the questions, according to the level and interests of the class. You could divide the class into groups to look at different questions. You may choose to analyze the questions together as a class so that you can discuss any difficult vocabulary.

It might be an idea to ask the students to underline the verbs from Ex 2.1 that they notice in each of the questions, to focus their thinking.

Answers:

1.   **a.** Answer should describe the properties of microorganisims that cause food spoilage.
    b. Answer requires food spoilage to be defined, followed by a description of how microbes cause food spoilage.
    c. Answer should state the different methods of reducing or preventing food spoilage.

2. Answer should focus on why and how livestock contribute to the welfare of the poorest people in developing countries.

3. Answer should focus on definitions of breed, breed substitution, crossbreeding and within-breed selection; examples should be given of how these cause genetic change.

4. Answer requires a comparison and contrast (similarities and differences) of the different feed resources for ruminants and non-ruminants. Evaluate these resources in order to answer the second part of the question.

5. Answer should include definitions of free trade and international economic growth, and a discussion of whether international economic growth is a consequence of free trade.

6. Answer requires definitions of international aid and global development and an analysis of whether or not global development can only take place if international aid exists.

7. Answer requires an explanation of the nature and structure of north–south relations, and whether such a structure has a negative effect on the development of less-developed countries.

8.   **a.** Answer requires a concise explanation of the need for quality control, quality assurance and quality management components within software quality systems.
    b. Answer requires an evaluation of the role and importance of software inspection for quality systems.
    c. Answer requires an explanation of the ways in which 'quality standards' are connected to software quality systems.

9. Answer requires a description of the techniques, how they work and an evaluation of their effectiveness in minimizing the wastage of irrigation water in horticultural production.

10. Answer requires a discussion of the impact of global warming on the ecology of the world, and what this means for the future.

11. Answer requires a brief overview of different ways to promote human development, followed by an evaluation of the possible contributions of the promotion of economic growth to this. This is followed by a conclusion as to whether this promotion is the best way. The writer needs to argue his/her stance.

12. **a.** Answer requires a definition of what the writer means by markets, and then an evaluation of their efficiency.

    b. Answer requires the application of the discussion from 12a to financial markets since 2008, considering whether the points made there apply to or can be exemplified by this particular time period.

13. Answer requires that the writer constructs an argument to show that he/she agrees or disagrees with the statement, having first defined the parameters of the terms used in the statement.

3.3 This activity gives students practice of the pre-writing process.

Study skills: Estimating word counts

You may like to show students how to estimate the number of words they have written by counting the number of words in three lines of text, dividing it by three and then multiplying it by the number of lines they have written. This is particularly useful for writing to set word counts in exams.

Task 4 | Writing your essay

For lower-level students, or to save time, it may be wise to ask them to read Text 4c for homework in preparation for the timed writing assignment in class. This will enable them to focus on the writing when working on their essay, rather than also worrying about their reading comprehension. Highlight that they will be able to look at the text when they write their essay in class.

For higher-level groups, you might prefer to incorporate reading the text into the time allocated for writing the essay in this task.

4.1 This task encourages students to reflect on what they already do and consider some new strategies they could try for writing in an exam. You could ask the students to read through the tips individually and put a tick (✔) next to the things that they already do, before discussing their ideas in pairs or small groups.

    Note: Tip number 8 refers to *linking words,* which will be covered in more detail in Unit 7.

4.2 It is worth spending some time discussing with students how they might approach this question. It asks students to describe the potential benefits of telemedicine in preventing and curing disease, and to discuss whether more potential applications will be found in preventing disease than curing it.

4.3/
4.4

The students should be familiar with brainstorming and organizing ideas by this stage. Refer back to the notes on setting up these activities in Unit 2, Task 1 if necessary.

Study skills: Double spacing

You might like to suggest that students make their writing double-spaced, particularly when writing in exams. This will give them space to write in corrections and additions when they read through their essay.

Write your essay

Decide on an appropriate time limit for students to write their essay. Given that they have already completed their plan, this could be around 20 minutes, depending on the level of your students.

Giving feedback on timed writing

A suggested marking scheme is given in Appendix 4a on pages 50–52. It consists of a set of criteria divided into different levels. This will give students an idea of their strengths and weaknesses when writing in timed conditions. The criteria are divided into the following categories:

- appropriate incorporation of relevant content
- developing a clear line of argument and organizing ideas coherently
- thesis statement/stance/position of writer, i.e., the viewpoint that the writer takes on the topic
- range and appropriate use of vocabulary and grammar
- accuracy of grammar use
- communicative quality

Typically, a student who consistently achieves A grades for each criterion would be ready to study a linguistically demanding subject, such as economics or politics. A student who is between A and B would be ready to study a less linguistically demanding subject, such as computer science or construction management.

You may also wish to give more detailed comment on the students' scripts and ask for a second draft.

There are two further timed writing tasks in Appendices 4b and 4c on pages 53–54 that you can photocopy and give your students as appropriate during the course.

Unit summary

1

Possible answers:
a. You still have to analyze the title, brainstorm ideas, organize ideas, write a first draft, self-evaluate, revise the first draft – and finally get it marked (teacher feedback).
b. Edit the first draft and add any information that could improve the answer.
c. You need to look for key words.
d. A general statement about the topic, some information relevant to the specific question, a brief outline of what you will discuss, and a statement of your own viewpoint.
e. You need to check clarity of ideas, spelling and grammar.

2 There are so many possible answers for these sentences that it would be useful to discuss answers with the students and clarify which ones are the most appropriate.

Possible answers:

a. analyze, comment on, discuss; consider, evaluate, identify, outline

b. consider, compare, discuss, identify, outline, summarize, state

c. analyze, consider, define, describe, discuss, identify, outline/comment on, compare, contrast, evaluate

Timed writing grades

Name:

Essay:

A+	✔
All your main points are relevant. One or two of your minor points may be irrelevant. You have used the content appropriately.	
You have organized your ideas and developed your argument clearly, coherently and logically.	
Your thesis (viewpoint/stance) communicates your position clearly and is well presented and maintained, and sophisticated in places.	
You have used a wide range of vocabulary and grammatical structure with good control.	
You have made only one or two errors in grammar use, which do not interfere with comprehension.	
Your writing communicates your message fluently.	

A	✔
All your main points are relevant. Only a few of your minor points may be irrelevant. You have used the content appropriately, for the most part.	
You have organized your ideas and mainly developed your argument clearly, coherently and logically.	
Your thesis (viewpoint/stance) communicates your position to the reader clearly, and is well presented and maintained.	
You have used a wide range of vocabulary and grammatical structure with reasonable control.	
You have made only minor errors in grammar use, which do not interfere with comprehension.	
Your writing causes your reader few difficulties.	

PHOTOCOPIABLE

B	✔
Most of your main points are relevant. Some of your minor points may be irrelevant. Some of your main and supporting points may be confused. You may have used the content inappropriately, and you may not have sufficient content.	
Overall, you have organized your ideas well, coherently and clearly, but in some places your argument needs further development.	
Your thesis (viewpoint/stance) communicates your position to the reader, but this is not sufficiently well maintained throughout the essay.	
You have <u>either</u> been ambitious and used a fairly wide range of vocabulary and grammatical structure in your writing, which in some places needs further control, <u>or</u> you have used a limited range of vocabulary and grammatical structure well.	
There are some errors in your grammar use, which may very occasionally interfere with comprehension.	
Your writing communicates satisfactorily; there is some fluency.	

C	✔
Many of your main points are not relevant, and many of your points require further support with details.	
Your main and supporting points are sometimes confused.	
There is some evidence of coherent organization of ideas in your writing, but there needs to be further development of your argument.	
You have tried to communicate a thesis (viewpoint/stance) to the reader, but this is difficult to follow.	
A reasonable range of vocabulary and grammatical structure in your writing is evident, but more control is needed.	
There are frequent errors in your use of grammar, which sometimes interfere with comprehension.	
Your writing communicates, although there is some strain for the reader.	

PHOTOCOPIABLE

D	✔
It is difficult to identify your main points, and most of them are not supported.	
There is little evidence of any coherent organization of ideas or development of argument.	
It is difficult to identify a thesis statement that communicates your position to the reader at any point in the essay.	
A limited range of vocabulary and grammatical structure is evident in your writing, but a lot more control is needed.	
There are many errors in your use of grammar, which often interfere with comprehension.	
Your writing communicates, but requires effort by the reader.	

E	✔
There are few ideas, which are undeveloped, in your essay.	
There is very little evidence of coherent organization of ideas and development of argument in your writing.	
There is no attempt at a thesis statement that communicates your position to the reader.	
The range of vocabulary and grammatical structure used in your essay is very limited, with little control.	
There are very many errors in your use of grammar, most of which interfere with comprehension.	
Your writing communicates, but requires substantial effort by the reader.	

Teacher:

PHOTOCOPIABLE

Appendix 4b

Timed writing

Write an essay on the following topic:

The impact of on-screen violence is having a serious social effect on young people. Discuss.

You should try to write 300–400 words.

You may make notes here:

_____

_____

_____

_____

_____

_____

_____

_____

_____

_____

_____

_____

_____

_____

_____

_____

_____

_____

_____

_____

_____

PHOTOCOPIABLE

Timed writing

Write an essay on the following topic:

Traditional values in society are in danger of completely disappearing as a result of modern developments. Discuss.

You should try to write 300–400 words.

You may make notes here:

PHOTOCOPIABLE

5 Food security

In this unit students will:

- make decisions about what the essay title is asking them to do, and organize their ideas
- consider one approach to problem-solving in their writing
- learn how to end a paragraph with an effective concluding sentence
- practise effectively writing a conclusion

This unit will prepare the students to write an essay on the following topic:

There are many threats to global food supplies. Explain the problem, identify possible solutions, and assess the implications of implementing these solutions.

This unit gives students the opportunity to develop their awareness of patterns of organization by practising a pattern of *Situation–Problems–Solutions–Implications–Evaluation*. They should use information from Texts 5a–5d from the Source Book, and any of their own, to support the ideas in their essays.

Note: The final paragraph of Text 5b has been removed from the Source Book. This is because in *EAS: Reading*, which also refers to Text 5b, there is an exercise which requires students to rearrange this paragraph. It is not referred to specifically in *EAS: Writing*. You may wish to explain to your students that this is the reason the text may appear to end quite abruptly. For reference, this final paragraph is provided as a photocopiable handout (Appendix 5d) on page 67.

Task 1 Microskills: Organizing your essay – SPSIE

This task focuses on how a problem-solving approach can be translated into the organization of a text by considering the following:

Situation ▶ Problems ▶ Solutions ▶ Implications ▶ Evaluation
(SPSIE)

Briefly discuss the bullet points about problem-solving in academic life in relation to the students' study context, e.g., what type of problems they would need to explore, how they would find/ suggest solutions, and work out the implications. You may need to examine the word *implications* in more detail and elicit the need to look at short-, medium- and long-term effects of solutions, and their relative merits.

Students should be made aware of the importance of evaluation in all aspects of academic life, having first accumulated evidence to be able to make sound evaluations. They should also develop the language to be able to do this.

1.1   Students could share their ideas in pairs to explain how the organization pattern has been applied in the student text.

Highlight the fact that this organization can be used for any length of text, from a paragraph to a complete book.

Answer:
Situation: The writer is an international student living in Britain.
Problems: He/she finds it difficult to meet British people, make friends and practise his/her English.

Solutions: Join university clubs.
Implications: Will take up a lot of time.
Evaluation: Should help the writer make friends and improve his/her English.

1.2 You may need to encourage the students to think of an appropriate situation, using pair or group discussion. You could elicit some possible topics and write these on the board to get them started.

Ask the students to swap their paragraphs and see if they can identify the different elements within it. They should give each other feedback on whether or not they feel they have included everything required. You may like to ask one or two of them to read out their answers to the class and do the feedback as a plenary discussion.

Key writing skills: SPSIE approach to writing

It's important to highlight that the SPSIE approach is just one way of organizing a text and that they will come across many other patterns. Emphasize that, as they have seen so far in this unit, this approach can be used at the paragraph level through to a whole book.

1.3 Ask the students to read the text and to think about these questions:
- What is the problem?
- What is the solution?
- What are the implications of the solution?
- Is there an evaluation of the solution at the end?

At this stage, they should just underline the information they think will help them to answer these questions.

1.4 Students complete the flow chart using the information they have underlined in the text to help them. Emphasize that they should use note form rather than copying whole chunks of text.

Answer:

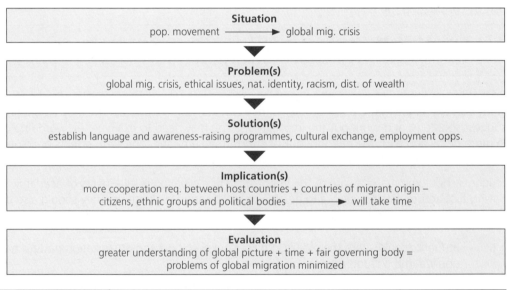

Situation
pop. movement ⟶ global mig. crisis

Problem(s)
global mig. crisis, ethical issues, nat. identity, racism, dist. of wealth

Solution(s)
establish language and awareness-raising programmes, cultural exchange, employment opps.

Implication(s)
more cooperation req. between host countries + countries of migrant origin –
citizens, ethnic groups and political bodies ⟶ will take time

Evaluation
greater understanding of global picture + time + fair governing body =
problems of global migration minimized

Study skills: Note-taking and quotations

At every stage of the course, students should be encouraged to take notes in note form rather than copying out whole chunks of text. It is then easier to write a summary in their own words and include an in-text citation in their notes, as they were shown how to do in Unit 2. This guards against any inadvertent plagiarism occurring when the time comes for them to use their notes to write their own essay.

1.5 You could ask the students to discuss their answers to this question in groups before sharing ideas in a whole-class plenary. Encourage the students to think about a solution for any further problems they identify and what the implications of them might be.

Possible answers:

A further problem might be: The organizational problems and financial implications related to greater cooperation; also the resistance of some governments to cooperate.

Further solution: The creation of organizations to implement new measures and to coordinate meetings.

Further implications/evaluation: There will be further economic and social problems before this can be done; financial aid will probably have to be obtained from the taxpayer.

Extension activity

If you feel that your students need further practice in approaching a problem in this way, you could ask them to think of a situation in their own country which has led to problems. Students write two short paragraphs and exchange these with a partner. They then complete a *Situation–Problems–Solutions–Implications–Evaluation* flow chart summarizing the content of the paragraphs.

1.6 The aim of this question is to raise students' awareness of appropriate language structures for evaluation.

Elicit the following:

- conditionals, e.g., *If X is done, then Y will happen.*
- *should*, e.g., *This solution should be effective in that it will …*
- use of modals and hedging, e.g., *This may lead to …*

Task 2 | Writing your essay

2.1 Students should now be familiar with the procedure of analyzing the essay title. They should look for key words and note that it is asking them to structure their essay using the SPSIE pattern they have been practising, with a logical flow from section to section.

You may like to discuss that they will need to include some kind of evaluation of these solutions, even if this is just a prediction. This is where they can give their own opinion, informed by what they have read in the source texts and elsewhere.

2.2 Encourage the students to brainstorm ideas under the headings of the SPSIE framework. They should also read through the source texts at this stage if they have not been using *EAS: Reading*. As there are four texts for this essay question in the Source Book, you may prefer to ask the students to read these for homework, ready to share their notes in the next class.

> **Study skills: Colour-coding**
> Students may find it useful to use different coloured highlighters to mark the parts of the texts they read that are relevant to different parts of their essay (i.e., different colours to indicate information relating to problems, solutions, implications and evaluation).

2.3 Students can work in small groups to complete the table.

Depending on the level of your group, you may also like to show or provide an example of a completed table on an OHT (or other visual medium) for them to compare with their own answer. This table can be found in Appendix 5a on pages 63–64. Emphasize to students that their notes may differ from the ones given and that there is no one right answer. Students should be able to make their own evaluations, as well as mentioning those in the texts.

2.4   Students should continue to follow the SPSIE structure for this essay.

Remind students about the work they have done on paragraph leaders in the previous unit and encourage them to include these in their plan. They will need to be selective, as they will not be able to include all of the points they have taken notes on in their essay.

Emphasize the importance of making sure that they answer the specific question that they have been asked. They should refer back to the essay title regularly throughout the planning process.

2.5/ 2.6   Students should be familiar with evaluating each other's plans at this stage of the course. Go through the focusing questions before they begin. Again, there should be emphasis on the content, language and flow for this particular pattern of organization.

2.7   **Writing the first draft**

Students write the first draft of their essay. They should aim for between 400 and 600 words.

2.8   Tasks 3 and 4 should be covered before the peer evaluation stage. Students read through their partner's essay and evaluate it using the peer evaluation sheet for this unit on page 88 of the Course Book.

Peer evaluation sheet: Unit 5

As in Units 2 and 3, it is advisable to check students' comprehension of the different sections of this form before they begin their evaluations. For more detailed information on the sections of the peer evaluation sheet, refer to the notes in Units 2 and 3.

Task 1

Section 1.1: Introduction

You may like to refer the students back to the work they did on writing introductions in Unit 2. Remind them that it is important that they move from general to specific ideas, that they clearly state the direction of the rest of the essay and that they include their thesis statement.

Section 1.2: Paragraphing and organization

You may want to refer students back to the work they did on paragraph leaders in Unit 3, as well as Task 3 of this unit.

Section 1.3: Incorporation of sources

Students should check that the information has been paraphrased accurately and the sources acknowledged appropriately.

Section 1.4: Conclusion

Task 4 of this unit focuses on writing conclusions. However, as mentioned earlier, asking the students to look at their partner's conclusion prior to this input should be a useful exercise.

Tasks 2 and 3

This should be familiar territory by this point. It might be an idea to refer the students back to the phrases on page 18 of the Course Book to remind them of the type of language they might use when giving feedback to their peers.

Task 3	**Microskills: Writing concluding sentences**

3.1 Lower-level students may need to be reminded that, to complete the task, it is not necessary to stop and check each word they do not know; the main focus needs to be on the last sentence.

However, for the third paragraph, you may want to clarify the meaning of the word *demographic* (connected to the scientific study of population numbers).

Answers:

Paragraph 1: The last sentence is a conclusion, or deduction, of the previous information.

Paragraph 2: The last sentence acts as a transition between the introductory paragraph and the following information in the chapter.

Paragraph 3: The last sentence predicts possible future consequences of rapid population growth.

Paragraph 4: The last sentence is a conclusion derived from the information given in the paragraph.

3.2 Encourage the students to use the answers from the previous activity to help them consider the general functions these sentences can have. They may also add their own ideas which may be different to the ones listed here.

Possible answers:

The concluding sentence in a paragraph can:

- summarize the main ideas of your paragraph
- restate the main topic
- be a conclusion derived from the information given in the paragraph
- predict the future
- suggest possible solutions
- link the ideas of the paragraph to the ideas of the following paragraph

3.3 You may find that you have already discussed this in the process of completing Ex 3.2. In any case, it is worth pointing out that individual concluding sentences can have more than one function.

Possible answers:

Paragraph 1 is a conclusion.

Paragraph 2 links ideas to the following paragraph.

Paragraph 3 predicts the future.

Paragraph 4 is a conclusion.

3.4 Students will come up with a number of variations for a suitable concluding sentence which they can compare with the possible answers below.

Possible answers:
Paragraph 1
- Thus, global warming has caused a significant amount of damage. (*summary*)
- Thus, action should be taken to stop the damage that is being caused by global warming. (*suggestion*)
- If action is not taken to slow down this process, then by the year 2050, the Earth will be a completely different environment. (*prediction*)

Paragraph 2
- Unless action is taken by the government to improve the situation, the quality of teaching will continue to deteriorate. (*prediction*)
- It is therefore suggested that the government takes appropriate action to improve the situation. (*suggestion*)

Paragraph 3
- Thus, changes in working habits and subsequent reductions in costs are due to progress in technological development. (*conclusion of information in the paragraph*)
- However, progress in technological development can also lead to negative consequences. (*transition to next paragraph about negative consequences*)

Methodology note: Adapting the material for lower levels
For lower-level groups, you could give students copies of the concluding sentences given as possible answers and ask them to match them to the paragraphs in this exercise. There is a photocopiable handout available for you to cut up in Appendix 5b on page 65.

Task 4	**Microskills: Writing your conclusion**

4.1 Be open to students' suggestions, but as a guide, the following points are important when thinking about the function of a conclusion.

Possible answers:
An essay conclusion:
- is a summary of the main ideas
- doesn't include new key points, but refers back to what has already been said
- can act as a prediction of future events related to the topic rather than future content of the essay
- draws on information from the whole essay rather than just one paragraph

Remind students that no new information should be given in the conclusion, only a discussion of what has already been said.

4.2 Before they read through the three conclusions, you may like to briefly elicit the types of things they would expect to read in a conclusion to an essay with the given title.

Possible answers:
Conclusion 1: A conclusion of information in the essay and a suggestion about what should be done.

Conclusion 2: A summary of the main body and a suggestion of what should be done.

Conclusion 3: A summary of the main body and a prediction of what might happen if things do not change.

Key writing skills: Writing conclusions

Ask students to read through the information given here and check their understanding. You may also want to highlight that a conclusion often mirrors the introduction to an essay, except that it will also often make predictions or suggestions for future action.

> **Methodology note: Optional activity**
> You may wish to show the conclusion in the photocopiable handout, Appendix 5c, on page 66. This is an example of a rather poor conclusion from a student, so it has not been included in the Course Book. A possible rewrite has also been given. Points you may wish to make:
> - It is a conclusion drawing on information from the essay.
> - It is generally not good practice to begin with *To conclude* or *In conclusion*.
> - The conclusion is not expressed with any force or clarity.

4.3 This task continues the topic with a focus on the structure of the conclusion.

Answer:
Sentence order: 2, 3, 1.

4.4 You can refer students to the information given in the *Key writing skills* section on this page to help them identify the function of each sentence.

Answers:
Sentence 2: This introduces the conclusion by giving a summarizing statement of the main points made in the essay. You might want to point out again that the student has begun with *To conclude*, which is not necessary. The position of the conclusion on the page, as well as the contents of the paragraph, will indicate that this is the purpose of this section of their essay. This sort of phrase is therefore redundant.

Sentence 3: Suggestions/recommendations for action.

Sentence 1: A prediction based on the information given in the essay.

4.5 **Answer:**
Sentence order: 3, 1, 4, 2.

Encourage the students to return to the conclusion they wrote for the essay in this unit. They should use the information they have learnt to help them do this. It might be an idea to ask them to work on these revisions in pairs or small groups.

Remind them that as well as looking at structure, they should ensure that they are not including new information. This is a common mistake.

Key writing skills: Concluding paragraphs

This summarizes the information covered in Ex 4.1 and throughout the rest of this task.

Remind students that the *Key writing skills* sections of each unit are very useful for revision purposes.

1

	Skill	Task/ exercise
a.	Make decisions about what the essay title is asking you to do, and organize your ideas.	Task 1
b.	Consider one of the ways to approach discussions of problems in your writing.	Tasks 1 and 2
c.	Learn how to end a paragraph with an effective concluding sentence.	Task 3
d.	Practise effectively ending an essay with a conclusion.	Task 4

2 Students could compare their answers with other students and to the suggestions given here.

Possible answers:

a. Each paragraph in an academic essay should have a concluding sentence which summarizes the main point of the paragraph and might evaluate the ideas within it and/or signal what will follow in the next section.

b. If you are discussing solutions to problems, you should also consider the implications of these and comment on how effective they may be.

c. The conclusion to your essay should summarize the main points you have made, refer to any future action needed or make a suitable prediction and move from a specific statement to a more general statement.

d. It should not include any new ideas.

Appendix 5a

Situation	■ Major issues of food security due primarily to population expansion and climate change (Text 5a) ■ Increased global wealth also creates higher demand (Text 5b) ■ ' … more food will need to be produced from the same amount of (or even less) land' (Godfray et al., 2010) (Text 5b, lines 113–114)
Problem	■ Threat to global food supplies (Text 5a) ■ Shortages of water and land (Text 5a) ■ Increased competition for land/water (Text 5a) and energy (Text 5b) ■ People in less-developed countries (will) suffer more (Text 5a) ■ Agricultural/ecological diversity is threatened by overproduction of some crops (Text 5a) ■ Health issues as a result of changes in ecosystems (Text 5a) ■ Overfishing (Text 5b) ■ Competition for resources from biofuel production (Text 5b) ■ Agricultural land has been taken over by urbanization and also lost its fertility (Text 5b) ■ According to World Bank, 70%–100% more food needed by 2050 (Text 5b) ■ There are significant 'yield gaps' in agricultural production (Text 5c) ■ Risks associated with investment are high (Text 5c)
Solutions	■ Education (Text 5a) ■ Research (Text 5a) (e.g., into varieties with high yields (Texts 5c and 5d) and better storage solutions (Text 5d)) ■ Increasing food yields in a sustainable way (Text 5a) ■ Reducing waste (Text 5a) ■ Better organization of supply chains (Text 5a), including better storage and transport (Texts 5c and 5d) ■ Global integration of approach (Text 5a) ■ Increase access to technical knowledge/skills for farmers globally (Text 5c) ■ Solutions are region-specific (Text 5c) ■ Carefully designed/implemented food subsidies (Text 5c) ■ Encouraging 'regional specialization in the production of the locally most appropriate foods' (Godfray et al., 2010) (Text 5c, lines 101–102) ■ Land rights need to be addressed by governments, particularly in poorer countries (Text 5c) ■ Better access to information and communications in developing countries (Text 5c) ■ Models to predict interaction between all these variables (Text 5c) ■ Research into genetic modification of key crops and animal cloning (Text 5d) ■ Increasing costs of food to better reflect actual costs of production (Text 5b) ■ Promotion of a vegetarian diet or focus on grass-fed livestock (Text 5d) ■ Consideration of potential for increasing focus on aquaculture (Text 5d)

PHOTOCOPIABLE

Implications	■ Better diet/nutrition for people in less-developed countries (Text 5a)
	■ 'Yield gaps' will close (Text 5c)
	■ Investing in agriculture will increase overall economic growth (and vice versa) (Text 5c)
	■ Better understanding and management of globalization in general and how it impacts on food production (Text 5c)
	■ If land rights are fair, people more likely to invest in (sustainable) development of their own land/agricultural business (Text 5c)
	■ Better access to information/communications will enable producers to have more confidence in market demand and know what current market prices are (Text 5c)
	■ Ethical concerns about cloning of animals for increased production
	■ Increased food costs may lead to lower amounts of waste in developed countries (Text 5d)
	■ Better education could also result in reduced waste (Text 5d)
Evaluation	■ Increased production could also lead to environmental implications such as an increase in greenhouse gases – therefore, all solutions need to be sustainable (Text 5c)
	■ Reducing waste is a key factor and, by doing this, food production and consumption could become more balanced across the world (Text 5a)
	■ Focusing on sustainability is the key message: 'The goal is no longer simply to maximize productivity, but to optimize across a far more complex landscape of production, environmental and social-justice outcomes' (Godfray et al., 2010) (Text 5d, lines 279–283)

Appendix 5b

Photocopy and cut up the items below along the dotted lines. Give one full set to each group of students. They work together to match the sentences to the paragraphs.

Thus, global warming has caused a significant amount of damage.

Thus, action should be taken to stop the damage that is being caused by global warming.

If action is not taken to slow down this process, then by the year 2050, the Earth will be a completely different environment.

Unless action is taken by the government to improve the situation, the quality of teaching will continue to deteriorate.

It is therefore suggested that the government takes appropriate action to improve the situation.

Thus, changes in working habits and subsequent reductions in costs are due to progress in technological development.

However, progress in technological development can also lead to negative consequences.

PHOTOCOPIABLE

Conclusion needing improvement

To conclude, searching for an ideal world is the main thought that occupies the minds of most people in developing countries, because they are living in such a difficult situation compared with the developed countries. These people know that it would not be an impossible achievement if there were no debts and no unfair constitutions, with no interference in their internal problems. They consider that there will be a day when money and power will not be considered the most important aspects of life.

Possible rewrite

Due to the difficult circumstances in which many people in developing countries live, many are searching for an ideal as represented by life in more developed countries. They are aware that an improvement in living standards would not be impossible to achieve if it were not for the issues discussed above, such as outside interference, unfair debt problems and inappropriate institutions of government. Despite an awareness of these issues and, in particular, the destabilizing influence of power and money, there is an optimism that this will one day no longer pose an obstacle to the fulfilment of their dreams.

PHOTOCOPIABLE

Appendix 5d

Recent studies suggest that the world will need 70% to 100% more food by 2050 (World Bank, 2008; Royal Society, 2009). Major strategies for contributing to the challenge of feeding 9 billion people, including the most disadvantaged, therefore need to be explored. At the same time, the combined role of the natural and social sciences in analyzing and addressing the challenge of feeding the poorest must be prioritized. Particular emphasis should be given to sustainability. Only when this has been fully established might a global catastrophe be avoided.

PHOTOCOPIABLE

6 Human resource management

In this unit students will:

- practise writing short and clear definitions
- write extended definitions
- develop their skill in supporting and exemplifying their ideas

This unit will prepare students to write an essay on the following topic:
To what extent does human resource management need to play a formal role in companies?

You may wish to spend time with the students discussing how they should respond to a 'To what extent' essay, i.e., that it is a discussion of the role(s) of human resource management (HRM), into which they should interweave their arguments for their viewpoint (i.e., do they think that HRM needs to play a formal role or not; if yes, why?/if not, why not?).

You may wish to give them a copy of the photocopiable handout in Appendix 6a on page 76 to help them decide on their viewpoint. Remind them that their views can be as strong as they like, as long as they argue their point with evidence. They should also remember to consider the opposing view, and provide arguments against this.

Students should use information from Texts 6a and 6b on human resource management in the Source Book, pages 40–44.

Task 1 Analyzing the question

The students go through the process of analyzing the question, brainstorming ideas and organizing these into a coherent order. They should also write out a brief plan at this stage. They will have a chance to revise and add to this later, before writing their essay.

1.1–1.3 By now, the students should be more independent in the planning stage of writing, so it may not be necessary to go through the answers question by question for Ex 1.1–1.3. You may want to just check how far they have got with their plans to ensure that they are on track.

Task 2 Microskills: Writing short definitions

2.1 Students should be able to point out that the verb *teaches* is only a different form of the word that is being defined, *teacher*. Thus, it is not a suitable definition, since if the reader does not know the word *teacher*, he/she will probably not know the verb *teaches*.

2.2 It is common to define a word in the following cases:

- when there are a number of possible definitions of a word and the writer wants to clarify which one he/she is referring to
- if the writer is including an item of key terminology and needs to demonstrate to the reader (a teacher or examiner) that they fully understand this concept
- when a writer is writing for a readership outside his/her subject area (It would be worth pointing out that when a writer is writing for his/her own community of scholars, there are generally common views about certain terms, which therefore do not need defining.)

2.3/ 2.4 Students will need to keep in mind the points raised in the previous exercise to complete these tasks. The points made are also summarized in the note in Ex 2.4.

Answers

1. no – *gene* is a basic concept in genetics

2. yes – the term *nurture* has a specialized meaning in context which needs explaining

3. yes – first-year undergraduates would not necessarily be expected to understand the term *migration* in context

4. yes – multiple definitions of *education* would be required

5. no – the specialist readership of such a journal would be expected to understand the term *globalization*

6. yes – this is a highly specialized area and the readership cannot be expected to already understand the term *particle physics*

7. no – *desertification* is a basic concept in geography

8. yes – *skimming* is a specialized term within English-language education which would need to be explained to a non-specialist reader

2.5 This would be an appropriate moment to revise the sort of language that is used when writing definitions. It is important to emphasize:

- that the definition should acknowledge that there are other possible definitions of the same word (e.g., by using phrases like *may be defined as* or *can be used to describe*, rather than *is*)
- the use of the relative pronoun

Possible answers:

1. *Globalization* may be defined as the intensification of economic, political, social and cultural relations across borders.

2. *Developing countries* can be defined as those countries which were previously colonized. **Note:** This is a good example of a definition which only includes one possible aspect of the definition of the term.

3. The term *subsistence farming* can be·used to describe contexts in which rural communities have grown their own food.

2.6 **Possible answers:**
Formal definitions

1. A *university* may be defined as an educational institution where students study for degrees and where academic research is done.

2. *Research* can be defined as the detailed study of something in order to find new facts.

3. A *library* may be defined as a place where books, journals and documents are available for people to look at or borrow.

2.7 **Answers:**
Naming definitions

1. An educational institution where students study for degrees and where academic research is done may be defined as a *university*.

2. The detailed study of something in order to find new facts may be defined as *research*.

3. A place where books, journals and documents are available for people to look at or borrow may be defined as a *library*.

Students may, of course, come up with suitably worded alternative definitions. Compare the two ways of writing definitions to make sure the students are able to do Ex 2.8–2.10.

2.8 **Answers:**

1. N
2. F
3. N
4. F

2.9/ Students work on these definition tasks individually. Discuss as a class. Emphasize how
2.10 using formal and naming definitions adds both authority and variety to essays. For Ex 2.9, you may wish to show the text on an OHT (or other visual medium) and ask students to come up and underline the definitions.

Key writing skills: Formal and naming definitions
It is worth spending time explaining how to write formal and naming definitions and giving the students some practice. They will need the ability to write accurate definitions on their courses.

Task 3	Microskills: Writing extended definitions

3.1 The students will probably need prompting to come up with ideas. You could give one example and get them to discuss in pairs to come up with more. You might want to look at the first extract in Ex 3.2 to elicit how it is done there (using an example, before discussing further ideas).

Answers:
A definition can be extended by giving:
- examples
- further details
- more specific detail about general information already given in the short definition
- further definitions of words used in the short definition
- advantages or disadvantages of an aspect of the concept being defined

3.2 **Answers:**
Extract 1: This paragraph has been extended with an example. Note the use of *refers*.

Extract 2: This paragraph has been extended with specific information about governmental loans – that is, the difference between these and commercial loans. There is also an indication of one of the positive aspects of such loans.

3.3   Point out the value of being able to define your area of study.

Answers:

1.   **Extract 1:** anthropology
     Extract 2: physics

2.   Subjects are becoming more specific. Also, when describing your subject, it is useful to situate it within a broader area of study, as it is more likely that people will be familiar with this than with your particular specialism.

3.4   This definition has been extended by using further definitions of an important word in the short definition, as well as a list of the topics covered by psychology. As it then goes on to explain the first of these topics in more detail, we can assume that it will continue with an explanation of the rest of the topics.

3.5   Students write an extended definition of their subject. The aim of this task is to give students practice in an area that interests them.

3.6   The paragraph is from Text 6b on page 43 of the Source Book, to help students focus on the essay topic, and is a good model of how a writer can discuss different viewpoints in their writing, and comment on them.

Answers:

1.   There are four definitions of the term *international HRM* or *IHRM*.

2.   *has been defined as; was essentially concerned with; agrees with but replaces; sees the three main issues as*
     It is worth spending time analyzing these definitions (shown on an OHT or other visual medium, for example) and looking at how the references and the language for introducing definitions have been integrated. Note also the use of the present perfect in the first definition.

3.   As IHRM is the main topic of the book, the writers thought it necessary to define the parameters of the discussion by examining different definitions in order to avoid misunderstandings. They focus here on giving some recent 'traditional' definitions which are concerned with expatriation.

4.   The writers introduce an alternative view to show that there is not full agreement and to set the context of his/her discussion.

5.   The paragraph leader introduces the idea that there is no single consensus about the term *IHRM*, thus anticipating the discussion of the definitions.

6.   The concluding sentence contextualizes the debate in connection with a related field in a global context, bringing to the fore the idea discussed that HRM practices can differ.

3.7   Tasks 3.6 and 3.7 should help students understand why it is important to include definitions in their writing. These tasks emphasize that there can be a range of definitions according to both historical and geographical contexts. They also give students practice of the use of in-text referencing and appropriate language to introduce definitions.

Answers:

1.   The main focus is on more recent definitions of IHRM developed in the light of globalization.

2.   By discussing the definitions that focus on the relationship between global and local management structures, and the cultural challenges.

3.8 It's worth giving the students some time to digest and discuss the information from these extracts and consider how they will use it in their own essay. Encourage them to re-read the specific essay question they have been asked and see how they can fit the points here into the plans they have been working on. Elicit ideas from the students.

Answers:

a.–b. Answers depend on students according to their particular essay focus and planning. Students may be tempted to repeat the discussion of the original texts, so you may wish to remind them to avoid this.

If they find this difficult, encourage them to read through the source texts again and highlight the key terms. They can then consider whether these will be useful for their own essays.

Task 4	**Microskills: Paragraph development – exemplification and support**

4.1 You may expect to elicit ideas such as examples, data, evidence from sources and detailed explanations.

4.2 Explain to students that they can ignore the sentence markers (a, b, c, etc.) for the first reading.

Answers:

1. The main idea is how technological and political changes have impacted on all aspects of cultures related to television (including the industry and viewers' habits).

2. The writers have given examples of how and where such changes have taken place.

3. By explaining details that the reader can relate to and using markers such as *first*, *second*.

4.3 Depending on the level of your group, it might be best to build up the questions about this paragraph leader on the board. Encourage the students to think about what they *don't* know about the topic being introduced in this sentence and what they would hope to find out about in the rest of the paragraph.

It may be an idea to continue working as a whole class for the remaining exercises based around this first text, before moving into groups and, finally, individual work for the analysis of the two further texts that follow in Ex 4.6 and Ex 4.7.

Possible answers:

- Why have these changes occurred?
- How have they occurred?
- Where have they occurred?
- What aspects of the televisual landscape have been transformed?
- How have aspects of the televisual landscape been transformed?
- Why have aspects of the televisual landscape been transformed?

You may like to point out that they can think in terms of the *wh~* question words and *how* to help them think about possible supporting details that might be included.

4.4   Some students may need help with this, as the answers demand some careful reading.

Emphasize that the writer has anticipated some of the questions that the reader may ask as they are reading and ensured that these are answered in a logical manner.

Answers:

1. **b:** the number of countries with broadcasting systems and the number of televisions available on which to watch their output has steadily risen
    e: governments have increased funding for TV companies

2. **b:** the number of televisions has risen
    c: there are more televisions in the world
    d: there are more terrestrial channels in the world

3. **f:** potential output of national television has risen
    h: higher demand for television imports

4. **g:** emphasizes the lack of the corresponding increase in national TV industries in relation to the expansion of output
    h: explains why there is an increase in television imports

4.5   **Answers:**

1. Sentence *g* explains one of the reasons why TV has become globalized: national TV industries are unable to fill all of the available broadcasting slots.

2. Sentence *h* is the concluding sentence in the paragraph. It summarizes the main idea of the paragraph: the ability to broadcast more television in countries around the world has increased the need for TV programmes to be bought and sold globally.

4.6   If you worked through the exercises based on the previous text as a class, you may like to ask the students to work in pairs or small groups to analyze this second paragraph from Text 5b in the Source Book.

Answers:

1. The topic of the paragraph is the relationship between global food prices and changes in the availability of food for a certain sector of the world population.

2–3.   Below are some examples of questions, all of which are answered by the writer:
    How are patterns in global food prices indicators of how the availability of food changes?
    Why are patterns in global food prices indicators of how the availability of food changes?
    What are the patterns?
    What examples of this relationship are there?
    What is the impact on people who do not have access to world markets?

4. a. Sentence *e* provides an example of the impact of an increase in food prices, a comment by the writer that there need to be other stimuli for food production (encouraged by governments and other organizations) in order to achieve a higher level of equality of access to food. Thus, the writer is emphasizing his/her concern about global food distribution.

    b. Sentence *f* also contains a comment that traditional staple food sources are not increasing, as the population is growing, from which the reader can infer that poorer members of the population will suffer.

    c. Sentence *g* presents another argument for not relying on food prices as an indicator of food availability.

4.7 If you have worked as a whole class for the previous exercises, or encouraged the students to work in pairs or groups, you may like to ask them to work individually for this final paragraph analysis task before checking answers in a plenary.

Answers:

1. The topic is the relative absence of biogas systems in the United States.

2. Some possible questions are:
   - Why are biogas systems rare in the United States?
   - Where in the United States are there any biogas systems?
   - What type of biogas systems are these?

3. Yes – the above questions are answered.

4. **a.** Sentence *d* mentions reasons why biogas systems are rare.

   Sentence *f* is a transition sentence, which moves the discussion to potential areas of development for biogas systems.

   b. Sentence *h* is a concluding sentence, suggesting how the United States could benefit from using biogas.

Key writing skills: Thinking critically

Critical reading and thinking skills are key factors in successful academic writing in most English-speaking universities. However, it is possible that less emphasis is placed on these in academic environments in other cultures. It is worth being aware that some students may initially struggle with these concepts.

Encouraging students to think in terms of *What? Who? Where? When? Why? How?* should help to train them in this kind of critical engagement.

Task 5	Using examples to develop your ideas

**5.1/
5.2** Encourage the students to look back at the extracts in this unit to find examples of these expressions. Elicit some ideas from the students and feed in additional items.

Possible expressions:
- an (a good) illustration of this
- an example of this can be seen in
- for example
- for instance
- a case in point
- such as

Make sure that the students note down these expressions, as they will need them to complete the next task.

5.3 **Answers:**

1. For instance/For example; For instance/For example
2. a case in point
3. A good illustration of this
4. such as
5. A good illustration of this

Task 6	**Writing your essay**

6.1 Elicit from students how they will improve their essays with definitions and support for their ideas.

Writing the first draft

Students write the first draft of their essay. They should aim for between 400 and 600 words.

6.2

Peer evaluation sheet: Unit 6

The peer evaluation sheet for Unit 6 includes questions reflecting the microskills covered in this unit, as well as the general ones on organization and structure.

See notes on peer evaluation in Units 2, 3 and 5 for further detail on this.

You will see that this peer evaluation sheet is longer than those that have been used previously as the students should now be able to review many different aspects of their partners' work.

You could consider asking the students to use these evaluation sheets to review their own draft and then revise it accordingly, before moving to the peer evaluation stage. This should encourage them to become more independent and able to judge their own writing more critically. It also highlights the fact that revision and redrafting are not single stages in the writing process and that they can both be returned to several times before the essay is ready to submit.

Unit summary

1 As this question encourages students to use their own voice (for explaining to another student), answers depend on students. Accept all reasonable answers.

2 **Answers:**
  a. *Firstly* is a chronological marker.
  b. *There have been several surveys which indicate* is a useful expression to introduce evidence based on statistical data.
  c. *A case in point is* introduces an example.
  d. *This is due to* introduces a supporting fact.

3 Encourage students to use what they have learnt about paragraph leaders and paragraph structure while completing this exercise.

If you have suggested that students keep a diary of their learning during the course, this might also be a good opportunity to remind them of these.

	HRM *does* need to play a formal role in companies	HRM does *not* need to play a formal role in companies
Agree		
Disagree		
Reasons		

PHOTOCOPIABLE

7 Sustainable fashion

In this unit students will:

- analyze essay titles and decide on appropriate organizational patterns
- consider the development of cause-and-effect relationships in their writing
- include statistics to support their ideas

This unit will prepare students to write an essay on the following topic:
The fashion industry poses a serious threat to the environment. A higher level of sustainability in materials production is the key solution. Discuss.

Task 1 Analyzing the question

1.1/
1.2
Students should be familiar with this procedure by now. Feed in ideas from below as needed, after looking at what they have come up with.

Answers:
There are three parts to this question: two statements and a word (*discuss*). Students may need to assimilate the content of the two statements, and to think about how they need to respond to this type of essay question.

Key words are: *fashion industry, serious threat, environment, higher level, sustainability, materials production, key solution, discuss*

A logical way to organize their ideas would be:

- a discussion of how the fashion industry threatens the environment and to what degree (cause and effect)
- a discussion of possible solutions, including a higher level of sustainability in materials production (point out that while this one is mentioned in the question rubric, it is probably not the only solution)
- an evaluation of the solutions with an argument as to which is the best one: this may be a higher level of sustainability, or it may be another (as long as the student argues strongly for this)

1.3 Students should note ideas from the texts as well as their own ideas.

Task 2 Microskills: Organizing your essay – cause and effect

The aim of this task is to raise students' awareness of various ways of organizing an essay of this type. Remind students of the SPSIE structure that they looked at in the previous unit. Explain that they will now be looking at a different organization pattern that can be useful for this type of essay question.

2.1 This activity aims to encourage the students to consider how this type of organization might work. They should look back at the ideas they have organized in Task 1 and consider how they could fit into this type of structure.

Answers
1. Students may contribute ideas such as reasons how and why the fashion industry poses a threat to the environment.
2. Students may contribute ideas such as a discussion of potential solutions, evaluating which could be the most effective.

2.2 Highlight that the essay they are going to analyze is answering a different question to the one that they will work on, but that the structure here is also divided into two parts. Analyzing the purpose of each paragraph in this example should help the students to understand how this type of structure works in practice.

Answers:
1. introduction to topic (moving from general to specific ideas)
2. situation (patterns of holidaymaking)
3. effects of tourism (problems)
4. effects of tourism on environment
5. effects on government (action to oppose the threat of tourism)
6. evaluation of action
7. conclusion/summary of main body

2.3 **Answers:**
1.–2. There are two main points to elicit here:
- The writer has only really addressed part of the question; he/she has not discussed the positive effects, so the essay is not balanced.
- Some students may say that the writer did not need to discuss the solutions in such detail. However, as the essay title has the word *discuss* in it, an analysis of the problems and possible solutions shows a higher-level approach to the task.

3. Other questions students can ask to evaluate the essay's success might include:
- Does the introduction contain a strong thesis statement with the writer's viewpoint, which gives direction to the rest of the essay?
- Has the writer suggested which solutions might be the most effective?

2.4 When discussing the ways a cause-and-effect essay can be developed, it is important to emphasize that the two ways presented in the Course Book are only to give students an idea of *possible* approaches; eventually, they will be able to be more flexible in their approach.

Providing initial help by introducing these possible structures will encourage weaker students to be more confident in their approach.

Point out that the Cause section and the Effect section in model 1 can be *more* than two paragraphs each, depending on their specific topic.

Similarly, there can be more than three cause/effect paragraphs in model 2.

Answers:
1. The essay seems to follow the second model more closely.
2. The choice of which model to use depends on the topic of the writing. The second model is more useful when the writer wishes to link the causes and effects very closely, whereas the first model is more useful when showing a close link is not so important.

2.5   This task raises awareness of suitable connectors for cause and effect. You could begin by eliciting the purpose of the phrases (introducing cause and effect) and the grammar of each item.

Answers:

1. *A consequence of* and *Owing to* are both compound prepositions and *This has caused* is a straightforward use of subject + verb followed by noun phrase.

2. Elicit the other connector in paragraph 1, *resulting in*, and then let the students find the others in paragraphs 3–6.

   3: *have caused* (line 2), *result of* (line 3), *at the expense of* (line 5–6), *due to* (line 9)
   4: *effect of* (line 1), *it causes* (line 1), *created by* (line 8), *has caused* (line 9), *gives rise to* (line 9), *causes* (line 10), *has resulted in* (line 12)
   5: *has prompted* (line 1)
   6: *is still causing* (line 4), *because of* (line 7)

3. Elicit other ideas for suitable connectors and write them on the board. You may need to prompt students to come up with variations on compound prepositions, such as *due to* and *because of*, and different verbs, such as *result in*. You may also want to prompt them to come up with the use of the conditional.

Key writing skills: Using multiple organization structures in your writing

It would be worth recommending that the students refer to the phrases and language they have been learning in Unit 7 as they write their essay for this unit. Point out that 'cause and effect' is a common structure for academic essays, but they will need to be careful in deciding which of the organization patterns they have looked at is the most appropriate for the specific question they are answering.

2.6   Go through the language to express cause and effect on pages 69–70 of the Course Book, drawing attention to the sentence structure. If short of time, this can be set for homework. You may wish to give your students further practice in using cause-and-effect expressions.

They can then use this to help them complete the exercise, connecting the ideas using a variety of these structures, along with the phrases from Ex 2.5. Encourage them to use a variety of structures in their answers.

Possible answers:

1. Since there is such a demand for air travel, the government is building more airports.

2. Due to the rising number of infected mosquitoes, malaria has become an even worse threat to health than in the 1990s.

3. Rain causes floods in many cities that have inadequate drainage and sewage systems.

4. Globalization is the major cause of cultural convergence.

5. The feeling of fear can have a substantial effect on levels of adrenalin in the body.

6. Inflation can result in higher levels of unemployment.

7. An arid climate will result in an increased need to irrigate fields artificially.

8. When there is a high rate of absenteeism in an organization, there is often low productivity.

9. A lack of plants can prompt major soil erosion in some areas.

10. There has been an increase in our interaction with satellites due to our use of mobile phones.

11. High birth rates can lead to overcrowding in some countries.

Methodology note: Practising specific structures

If the students have found Ex 2.5 and 2.6 difficult, it may be worth asking them to write a further sentence for each of the language structures outlined in the *Useful expressions to express cause and effect* boxes on pages 69–70. They could check each other's work in pairs before submitting their answers to you. The more confident the students become at using a variety of structures such as these, the more fluent their writing will become.

Task 3	**Writing your essay**

3.1   By now, students should be much more independent in their approach to essay writing and in the choices that they need to make to respond to the task.

However, it is worth spending time exploring how students can integrate the two organizational patterns of SPSIE and cause and effect (i.e., the causes of the threat by the fashion industry to the environment and the effect on the environment, and this then being the problem in an SPSIE pattern, with the emphasis on the most effective solution).

3.2/
3.3   Ask the students to read or re-read Texts 7a–7c in the Source Book (pages 45–54) as part of their preparation. You may wish to talk through the texts as a class.

The introduction to Text 7a offers an accessible summary of the issue, with the rest of the text exploring different aspects of the issue in more detail.

Text 7b discusses in more detail the impact on the environment of fashion materials, expressing the view that some so-called eco-products are not so environmentally friendly, and exploring the myth that animal skins are not sustainable materials, as well as giving examples of new kinds of materials.

Text 7c is also a good model of evaluating possible solutions, which leads to other potential problems (Section 5). Text 7c also offers a fairly detailed discussion of the feasibility of eco-fashion in the future.

It is hoped that, at this stage in the book, students are capable of extracting relevant information in the texts, and can make a good effort to express the content in their own words.

3.4   When students read through each other's essay plans, emphasize the need to look carefully at the structure their partner has chosen to use. It may not be the same as his/her own, but it needs to show that all parts of the question will be addressed.

Writing the first draft
Students write the first draft of their essay. They should aim for between 400 and 600 words. They should incorporate the feedback on their essay plan into their first drafts.

3.5
Peer evaluation sheet: Unit 7

As in Unit 6, the peer evaluation sheet here is longer than those for Units 2, 3 and 5. Students should now be able to review many different aspects of their partners' work.

| Task 4 | **Microskills: Using statistical facts** |

This section focuses on some further ways that information can be incorporated into an essay. This includes extrapolating information from non-text-based sources (e.g., graphs, charts, tables, etc.) and also looking at how students can extract key information from texts that are particularly dense with facts and figures.

4.1   Elicit students' ideas on the board: these are likely to include tables, bar charts and graphs.

4.2   You may wish to show the students examples of the range of newspapers in circulation to raise their awareness. Explain (if students are unaware) that broadsheets are newspapers printed on large sheets of paper, which have a more serious, formal tone than tabloid newspapers. Elicit students' responses on the board.

Possible answers:

1.   The decline, over 30 years, in the number of adults who read a national daily newspaper; the decline in circulation of the *Daily Mirror* and the *Daily Express*, partly due to the increase in the popularity of the *Sun*; the readership of the 'broadsheets' has been more stable than that of the tabloids.

2.   The decline in readership may be due to the increase in the number of free news websites, and the increase in the use of electronic media for distributing news; the stability of broadsheets is possibly due to the fact they contain more in-depth articles on a range of issues (political, cultural). Students may need to be prompted.

> **Study skills: Using statistics**
>
> It is worth highlighting that statistics can be useful for adding weight to arguments and providing evidence for the points students make in an essay. However, they should remember to be critical of the sources of these statistics and consider appropriate phrases to use if there is any doubt as to the validity of these figures.
>
> There is a weblink to a site highlighting how statistics can be misleading given on the *EAS: Writing* website.

4.3   It is important to emphasize the way that the writer has described the information in the tables. For example, in sentence 2 he/she writes: '… the proportion reading national newspapers *has fallen by approximately ten percentage points every ten years*.' He/she is not merely reporting the figures shown, but is interpreting and summarizing the information in a way that makes the key trends clear to the reader.

Answers:

1.   To give an analysis of the most 'interesting' or important information represented in the table, and to offer possible reasons.

2.   The decline, over 30 years, in the number of adults who read a national daily newspaper; the decline in circulation of the *Daily Mirror* and the *Daily Express*, partly due to the increase in the popularity of the *Sun*; the readership of the 'broadsheets' has been more stable than that of the tabloids.

This task aims to focus students' attention on how the different tenses can be used to relate trends, and positions the facts and figures they use in the past, present and future. It is worth highlighting that if the wrong tense is used, this can alter the significance of the statistic from the reader's perspective.

Answers:

a.   **1.** The estimated proportion of adults aged 15 and over in Great Britain who read a national daily newspaper <u>has been decreasing</u> over the past 30 years, from 72 per cent of adults in 1981 to 41 per cent in 2010, according to the National Readership Survey (Table 1). **2.** On average, since 1981 the proportion reading national newspapers <u>has fallen</u> by approximately ten percentage points every ten years.

3. The most commonly read newspaper in 2010 <u>was</u> the *Sun*, though readership has decreased from 26 per cent of adults who read newspapers in 1981 to 16 per cent in 2010. **4.** In fact, most tabloid newspapers <u>experienced</u> substantial falls in readership over this period. **5.** The *Daily Mirror* <u>suffered</u> the largest decrease, falling from being the most commonly read in 1971, when 34 per cent of adults read it, to 7 per cent in 2010. **6.** The *Daily Express* <u>has also suffered</u> a similar fate, falling from 24 per cent in 1971 to 3 per cent in 2010.

7. The readership of most other newspapers <u>has remained</u> stable, fluctuating by only one or two percentage points over the period. **8.** These <u>are</u> mainly the broadsheets, which have kept their smaller but more targeted audiences.

9. The decline in the proportion of those reading national newspapers <u>may be affected</u> by the availability of news websites which are free on the Internet. **10.** A recent survey by YouGov <u>asked</u> whether respondents would consider paying for access to online news sites. **11.** Only 2 per cent <u>stated</u> yes they definitely would, while a further 4 per cent said they would pay but only for special content, for instance content not available elsewhere. **12.** A further 6 per cent <u>stated</u> they might possibly pay for online content, while the majority (83 per cent) stated that they would not consider paying for access to newspapers online (YouGov, 2010b).

b.

Sentence	Verb(s)	Tense	Reason
1	*has been decreasing*	*present perfect continuous*	*describes an ongoing trend*
2	has fallen	present perfect simple	to show a situation that started in the past and continued until now, i.e., the drop in readership that started in 1981
3	was	past simple	to show a situation that was true in the past, but is not true now (it is finished), i.e., the most commonly read newspaper in 2010
4	experienced	past simple	to show a situation that was true in the past, but is not true now (it is finished), i.e., the fall in tabloid readership
5	suffered	past simple	to show an action in the past that has finished, i.e., drop in the *Daily Mirror* readership

6	has also suffered	present perfect simple	to show an action that started in the past and continued until now, i.e., drop in the *Daily Express* readership
7	has remained	present perfect simple	to show an action that started in the past and continued until now, with a result, i.e., stability in readership
8	are	present simple	to show current situation
9	may be affected	present simple passive voice with a modal	to show a possible reason
10	asked	past simple	to show an action in the past, at a particular moment, that is finished
11	stated	past simple	to show an action in the past, at a particular moment, that is finished
12	stated	past simple	to show an action in the past, at a particular moment, that is finished

4.6   Encourage the students to analyze the table carefully before they begin writing and write a brief plan of what they will include. Highlight that they need to be selective. It may also be worth pointing out that the topic sentence specifically refers to *differences*, so there is no need for them to consider the similarities between the age groups in this particular paragraph. It may work best for students to work in pairs as they do this exercise.

You can give students a photocopiable handout of a sample paragraph that can be found in Appendix 7a on page 85.

Possible answer:

Watching television has been a common pastime for decades and continues to be so in 2009/2010. The latest data from the *Taking part* survey show that watching television in their free time was still the most common activity reported by adults aged 16 and over in England (Table 2). Eighty-nine per cent of all adults watched television in their free time and it was the most popular activity for age groups from 35 upwards. However, for those aged 16–24, the highest proportion of respondents selected spending time listening to music (90 per cent). Those aged 25–34 reported spending time with friends and family as their joint top activity, along with watching television, with 85 per cent of respondents in this age group saying that they did these activities in their free time.

Overall, for adults aged 16 and over, spending time with family and friends was the second most popular activity at 84 per cent, listening to music came next at 76 per cent, and shopping was fourth at 71 per cent.

The overall averages also hide differences between the age groups for other activities. Comparing the 16–24 age group with those aged 65 and over, the activities which were reported less frequently as age increased were listening to music (90 per cent and 69 per cent respectively); Internet and e-mailing (79 per cent and 24 per cent); sport and exercise (63 per cent and 35 per cent); going out to pubs, bars or clubs (59 per cent and 33 per cent); and going to the cinema (72 per cent and 21 per cent). Again, comparing the youngest and oldest age groups, the activities which were reported more frequently as age increased were reading (53 per cent and 73 per cent) and gardening (16 per cent and 62 per cent).

4.7 This could work well as a group activity, with the students working together to consider how the information from this graph might be incorporated into their essay. Refer them back to the specific essay title so that they are clear on the type of information that will and won't be relevant. As always, they will need to be selective.

You could also encourage the students to look for other sources of statistical information that could be useful for their essay. It is worth emphasizing that they may sometimes choose to include a table, graph or bar chart in their essay, but they will always need to incorporate an interpretation of the key facts into the main text rather than expecting the graph or table to speak for itself.

The students should now be ready to revise their essays, considering the points they have covered in Task 4.

Unit summary

1 Encourage the students to discuss these points in pairs or groups outside the class.

Possible answers:

a. All paragraphs should start with a paragraph leader and end with a concluding sentence. However, the way that the content within them is structured will change according to the type of organizational pattern that is most suited to the question that the students are answering.

b. It is very important to cover all parts of a question. Students will lose marks if they don't, as it will not be considered to be a full answer. It is possible that they may identify, for example, more advantages than disadvantages, but they can comment on this and give their opinion on whether they think the situation is more beneficial or detrimental.

c. Students can be flexible with their plans in terms of how many paragraphs they use for each section. However, for many essays, they will need to ensure that they give balanced input on the different parts of the question they are answering.

d. Academic language is quite specific and there are many recognized phrases and expressions associated with different ways of putting arguments across. The more familiar students become with using the phrases, the more natural their writing will sound and the easier it will be to follow.

2 These answers, although fairly obvious, highlight some important issues.

Answers:

a. The decision on how to organize your essay should depend on the topic of the essay.

b. You need to plan your paragraphs and edit them after you have written your first draft so that each paragraph has a clear function.

c. It is important to answer the essay question fully and give a balanced answer. For example, if you are asked to discuss advantages and disadvantages, you should try to give equal attention to both sides of the argument.

d. You can use different patterns to organize your essays. As you become more skilled and confident, you can be more flexible.

e. If you are aware of, and able to use, common essay-writing expressions, it will make the ideas in your essay clearer and easier to follow.

Appendix 7a

There are certain noticeable differences in free-time activities between older and younger people in the UK. Firstly, listening to music appears to be of much greater interest to young people aged between 16 and 24 than any other age group. Ninety per cent of 16–24 year-olds reported that they did this, compared with just 69 per cent of people aged 65 and over. In contrast, people over the age of 45 reported spending significantly more time gardening than people under the age of 35, with only 16 per cent of 16–24 year-olds indicating that they did this in their free time. Another interesting difference is the number of younger people who said that they enjoyed going to the cinema as a leisure activity. This interest appears to tail off as people get older, with just 21 per cent of people aged 65 and over including it as a preferred pastime. Other activities which were reported less frequently as age increased were Internet and e-mailing (79 per cent and 24 per cent respectively); sport and exercise (63 per cent and 35 per cent) and going out to pubs, bars or clubs (59 per cent and 33 per cent). Older people reported spending more time reading (73 per cent) than in doing any of these activities. Thus, these examples suggest that as we get older, the way that we choose to spend our free time tends to change.

8 The Tipping Point

In this unit students will:

- analyze essay titles and decide on appropriate organizational patterns
- consider the development of compare-and-contrast relationships in their writing
- incorporate ideas from sources as quotations to support their ideas

This unit will prepare students to write the following essay, using Texts 8a–8e from the Source Book: *Compare and contrast the role of Innovators and Early Adopters with the role of the Early Majority in achieving commercial success. Relate your answer to Gladwell's theory of the Tipping Point.*

Task 1   Background reading

1.1   Students should now be familiar with reading a text with the specific purpose of finding relevant ideas for an essay, to support their own ideas and arguments.

Task 2   Analyzing the question

2.1   Students may need longer to do this than previously, as the title is more complex.

There are two main parts to the title. In many university departments, particularly business, marketing and management fields, it is common for essay questions to ask students to relate practice to theory. This question gives students practice with this.

The key words in this essay title are: *compare, contrast, role, Innovators, Early Adopters, Early Majority, commercial success, Gladwell's theory, the Tipping Point.*

2.2/
2.3   Elements of the two organization patterns covered in Units 6 and 7 can be incorporated into this essay.

Students will be expected to introduce both parts of the essay in the introduction, then develop the comparison and contrast of the two roles, with an evaluation of their relative importance in achieving success. A discussion of how this fits into the theoretical framework should follow, and at the end, an evaluation of the suitability of the theory for this situation.

2.4   Elicit from students ways of integrating discussions of theory and practice. For example, the link to theory can be woven into the discussion of the different roles, or it can follow the discussion of the roles, with explicit links being made back to the comparison and contrast.

Task 3	**Microskills: Organizing your essay – comparison and contrast**

Emphasize the importance of being able to make valid comparisons and contrasts in academic life, and that writing such a discussion can be part of an essay structure which might include SPSIE and cause and effect (e.g., comparison and contrast might be part of the evaluation of various possible solutions to a problem).

Methodology note: Peer teaching

You could take a fairly hands-off approach to this section and encourage the students to work together to make sense of this input.

One way to do this collaboratively would be to put the students into pairs and ask them to look at either the vertical pattern or the horizontal pattern and see if they can come up with an example of how this would work.

They then work with a pair who have been looking at the other pattern and explain to each other how the one they have focused on works.

3.1   This is a vertical pattern (apples are described, then oranges).

3.2   If the students have been working in groups, they could remain in their groups to rewrite the paragraph together.

Possible answer:
Apples are generally oval in shape, whereas most oranges are rounder. Apples range in colour from green to yellow to red, while the colour range of oranges is more limited, from vermilion to pale orange. The texture of apples is usually firm and sometimes even hard, but oranges are relatively soft.

Emphasize the fact that in a horizontal pattern, more 'contrast words' are needed. It might be useful to ask the students to identify the expressions for showing contrast in the possible answer you have given them for this exercise (i.e., *whereas, while, but*) before moving on to look at the expressions listed on pages 78–79 of the Course Book.

3.3   Monitor students as they write. For lower-level groups, it may be useful to quickly brainstorm some ideas about the things they could write about before they begin, or encourage them to work in pairs or small groups.

3.4   Check that students have correctly identified the pattern in their partner's essay before moving on to Ex 3.5.

3.5   Ask one or two students to write their paragraphs on the board or type them up to project on an OHP (or other visual medium), and ask the rest of the class to comment on them. Is it clear which pattern they have used?

Key writing skills: Common expressions and markers for comparison and contrast
You may like to ask the students to use the sentence frames given to write out some examples, substituting the 'X' and 'Y' for real items.

3.6   The students can refer back to the essay title and the notes they have made on their reading of the source texts and consider which of these expressions are likely to be useful.

Emphasize the point made in the introduction to this task that it is always better to express source material in one's own words, but particularly pertinent phrases or sentences can be quoted. Many students overuse direct quotations.

4.1   Text 8e contains a number of useful examples that students can use in their essay, while some of the earlier texts focus more on the theory of the tipping point and its development.

4.2   This is a good example of the type of sentence that students might be inclined to include as a direct quotation, as it makes a key point and is well written.

Possible answers:

1. Yes. The extract gives an example of a company that understood how to take advantage of the way that products can reach a tipping point in terms of sales. It used this understanding to create a successful advertising campaign.

2. It is very well written and succinct, so possibly not.

3. It could be included as a direct quotation as it is relatively short and will make an impact. It will therefore need to be written within quotation marks and cited appropriately.

Key writing skills: Using direct quotations

This section explains how direct quotations should be incorporated using an appropriate citation and quotation marks. Ask the students to identify the differences between the three ways shown here.

1. Sentences 1 and 2 use the verb *emphasizes* to introduce the quotation.

2. Sentence 1 begins with *As*, followed by *Gladwell*, and then the verb *emphasizes*, whereas sentence 2 begins with *Gladwell*, followed by the verb *emphasizes*, followed by *that*. Where a verb is used to introduce the quotation, it is made clear at the beginning of the sentence who originally said what is quoted (Gladwell), whereas in sentence 3, the original author is only stated as an in-text reference after the quotation. Where a verb has not been used, the quotation makes up the whole of the sentence. Elicit also the main differences between sentences that use a verb and those that do not.

3. Quotation marks.

4. A comma.

4.3   Refer students back to the work done in Unit 2. Elicit other verbs.

Possible answers:

acknowledge, argue, comment, describe, emphasize, explain, express, indicate, mention, note, point out, propose, remark, report, state, suggest

Remind students they can also use these words for introducing ideas as paraphrases.

4.4   Students practise the three different ways of incorporating quotations with the sentence given.

Possible answers:

- As Gladwell (2010) reports, '… there is a substantial difference between the people who originate trends and ideas and the people in the Majority who eventually take them up' (p. 197).

- Gladwell (2010) asserts that '… there is a substantial difference between the people who originate trends and ideas and the people in the Majority who eventually take them up' (p. 197).
- '… there is a substantial difference between the people who originate trends and ideas and the people in the Majority who eventually take them up' (Gladwell, 2010, p. 197).

Study skills: Using parts of sentences as quotations

This might be a good time to explain how students can use just part of a sentence as a quotation by including an ellipsis (…).

It may also be useful to show them how they can insert a word to clarify what the writer is talking about by using square brackets. For example, if the writer has used a pronoun to refer to something in a previous sentence or part of the sentence which the student doesn't want to include, they may need to exchange the pronoun for the noun it refers to, e.g., *Malcolm Gladwell (2010) reports that '… [Airwalk's] advertising was founded very explicitly on the principles of epidemic transmission' (p. 196).*

4.5   The main difference is that the quotations in the *Key writing skills* section on page 80 are integrated into the sentence, whereas the one in this task starts on the next line and is indented. Emphasize that if students want to use more than 40 words of text in a quotation, they should follow this convention.

Key writing skills: Including extended quotations
It might be an idea to show the students some other examples of extended quotations that have been used in academic writing so they can see how they are embedded into the text.

4.6/ 4.7   Students make their own choices of useful quotations; monitor their discussions, and elicit some examples in class discussion at the end. Elicit the reasons why they are useful for the essay.

| Task 5 | Planning and writing your essay |

5.1/ 5.2   As this is the last essay of the course, students should be encouraged to work independently of you, but with some help from their peers.

5.3

Peer evaluation sheet: Unit 8
This form is very similar to the one used in Unit 7, except there are questions to focus students' attention on whether the writer has used a horizontal or vertical pattern when comparing/contrasting, and included direct quotations appropriately.

Unit and course summary

You may wish the students to think about and discuss these questions in preparation for a class plenary prior to completing the *Assessing your progress* form on page 93 of the Course Book.

a Appendix

Assessing my progress (Course Book)

The aim of the activity in the Appendix of the Course Book is to encourage students to assess their progress in academic writing over the course. They should try to identify consistent patterns of strengths and weaknesses, as well as identifying areas where they have improved.

Some students may find this difficult to do at first, so you may need to give them some concrete examples of how to do this.

Students should fill in the table on page 93 of their Course Books.

At the end, have a plenary session in which each student states one or two areas that he/she is going to work on in the future to improve their writing.

This self-assessment can be done at a certain stage during the course or at the end.